the *L*OVERS' *guide*

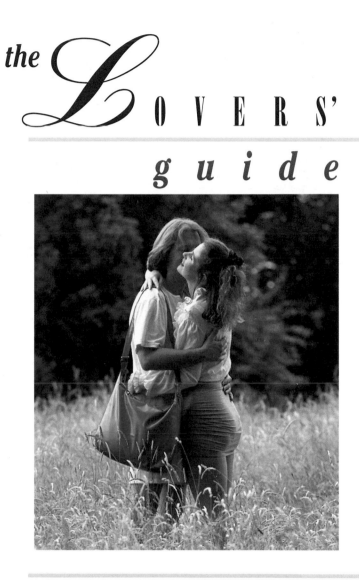

The art of better lovemaking

the *Lovers'* guide

The art of better lovemaking

Consultant DR ANDREW STANWAY

A·THOMAS·DUNNE BOOK

ST MARTIN'S
PRESS

Design by: Nigel Partridge

ISBN 0–312–10413–8
"A Thomas Dunne Book"

First published in Great Britain by Sidgwick & Jackson Limited.
First U.S. Edition: February 1994
1 3 5 7 9 8 6 4 2

AN EDDISON·SADD EDITION
Edited, designed and produced in association with
Lifetime Vision Limited by
Eddison Sadd Editions Limited
St Chad's Court
146B King's Cross Road
London WC1X 9DH

Typeset in Garamond by Axis Design, London
Origination by Mandarin Offset, Hong Kong
Printed by Bath Press Colourbooks, Glasgow

CONTENTS

$\mathcal{J}$NTRODUCTION

Lovemaking should not be confined to the bedroom, and lovemaking does not always need to involve intercourse. Just being together, talking and touching one another's bodies are sensual pleasures in themselves.

Sex is a subject which interests us all. Yet in our culture, it tends to be regarded as strictly private and confidential – something even to be kept secret, hidden and certainly not discussed. For this reason, it can be very difficult to learn about sex from first-hand experience.

THE LOVERS' GUIDE is intended for all the men and women who would like to know and understand more about sex – not from idle or unhealthy curiosity, but to ensure that they can give and receive in the context of a happy love life.

In this age of AIDS, too, it is vital that partners should be informed about sex – its pleasures and rewards, and also its possible risks and consequences. Together with THE LOVERS' GUIDE video series, this book is designed to help educate all lovers, including those in long-term relationships. It is important to remember, however, that no matter how well informed you are about sex, unless you are absolutely sure of your partner's sexual history, *you must always use a condom when you make love.* Only by being totally honest and realistic about your own activities, needs and fears can you and your partner take the right measures to protect each other effectively.

Better sex is not the key to a happy love life. But poor sex damages millions of relationships the world over. This is because sex is not a commodity in its own right. It takes place between two human beings who have past experiences, present realities, and different conscious – and unconscious – agendas. Sex can never be a simple physical act like walking down the street: it always carries deeper messages and meanings.

When the producers at Lifetime asked me to make THE LOVERS' GUIDE video series, I set out to create a modern document that would take all this into account. Obviously, the direct observation of real people actually having sex is not easy to achieve. But the advent of video made it possible to bring pictures into the privacy of our own homes, so that now – thanks to the considerable courage of the couples who agreed to appear – everyone can improve, or confirm, their personal knowledge of practical sexuality.

THE LOVERS' GUIDE on video is now distributed all over the world. Different countries have incorporated it into their particular cultures, in their own unique ways. Predictably, such an explicit and honest visual representation of sex has caused a stir wherever it has been shown. But millions of people have now seen the videos, and the feedback has been hugely positive.

"Thank you for giving me 'permission' to do things we'd been doing for years, but felt guilty and anxious about …" "Thank you for helping us feel better about ourselves by making us realize that what we wanted – but hadn't dared – to do is normal." "Please keep up the good work; it really got us talking like nothing else."

These are only some of the kinds of comments I get as I travel the world, listening to what people think and feel about THE LOVERS' GUIDE videos.

Video, though, is but one medium of communication. Therefore THE LOVERS' GUIDE has been made into a book for those who want to take the messages more slowly and thoroughly than the spoken word allows, and perhaps to turn to the videos for reference.

THE LOVERS' GUIDE book takes the same simple and straightforward approach to practical sex, preferred by most people. Lavishly illustrated, it is honest, open, explicit and pulls no punches. With greater knowledge and understanding of sexuality, with openness, trust and better communication between one another, every couple could build a more successful and lasting one-to-one relationship.

I hope that this book will help as many people as the videos have. In the book, as in the videos, personal experiences as extracts from conversation are included, and these retain the original, sometimes direct language used. These 'vox pops', along with the Question Time pages at the end of each chapter, bear witness to the reality of the experiences and problems described, and more importantly, to the efficacy of the solutions suggested.

By helping readers to know and understand one another's true feelings, I am sure THE LOVERS' GUIDE book will empower individuals everywhere to reach greater fulfilment in their sexual lives.

Dr Andrew Stanway
Consultant to THE LOVERS' GUIDE

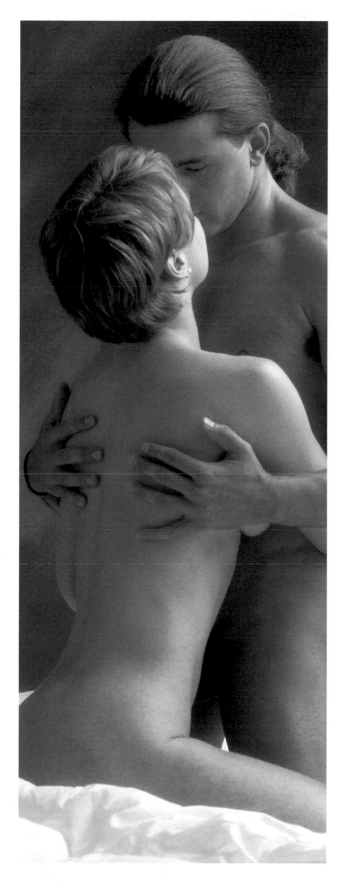

CHAPTER 1

UNDERSTANDING ONE ANOTHER

How to appreciate one another's

physical and emotional needs and

how to use this knowledge to help

overcome shyness and inhibition to

get the most out of your relationship.

COMMUNICATING ABOUT SEX

When I first moved in with Sean, it seemed like we just lived for sex. But after a few months, I secretly began to worry that I wasn't feeling satisfied, though I couldn't bring myself to talk to him about it, in case he got upset or angry with me. Then one night, when I wasn't feeling at all sexy when he wanted to make love, I just blurted it out, and told him that things had to change. That I wanted him to touch me, and masturbate me first. He put his arms round me and told me that he loved me. He knew something had been wrong, but didn't know what it was. You know, I was so relieved. Since then, we've talked about sex a lot – we even wrote a list of things to do, and I must say our sex life has improved.

ROSIE

For the majority of people, the greatest difficulty of their sexual life lies in communicating exactly what they feel, or want, to their partner. In fact, not communicating about sex lies at the heart of arguments and difficulties in many long-term relationships: countless surveys show that communication problems rank highest on the list of reasons people give for getting divorced. For a relationship to be truly fulfilling for both partners, one of the most important things is to feel that there is mutual understanding.

Talking about sex, however, is not easy – especially when it involves our very own, personal sexuality rather than sex in general. Sex is such a private subject that, even in many highly intimate relationships, couples feel awkward about revealing their sexual needs, desires and anxieties. But those who do manage to break down the barriers invariably find that the emotional side of their life together grows stronger, and that their lovemaking becomes much better.

LISTEN FIRST, TALK SECOND

Although most of us think of communication between two people as talking, it has more to do with listening. And listening construc-

Try to set aside a time to talk about, and listen to, one another. If it helps, choose a neutral location, such as a walk in the country, in which you can both feel relaxed.

tively can be very difficult to do, especially when the discussion is on a tricky subject like sex and relationships. The first thing we must do is to put our own ego to one side, so that we can be truly receptive to our partner. Too often, our own thoughts get in the way, so that we are not listening at all to what is being said. Although this problem can affect both men and women, more women complain that their partner does not understand them.

MAKE THE TIME

Be positive about communication – the earlier you start in your relationship the better for you both. All too often, something that has been bottled up by one partner suddenly gets thrown into an argument about a completely different subject: as a result, one of you can be so badly hurt that the subject becomes a 'no-go' area which is avoided in the future, and never discussed.

It is always worth investing time in a loving relationship. Try to set aside special occasions when you can both feel at ease to talk about your emotions and sexuality. Agree on a suitable location where you will both feel comfortable – perhaps on neutral territory such as a walk in the country, or at home with the telephone off the hook and a small drink to relax you.

Do not force the pace – you will not necessarily be able to approach every issue in one go – and if certain subjects become difficult for one of you, move on to another. Simply dumping your

Most men like their partner to take charge of lovemaking, and be on top occasionally. Many women, however, are inhibited about being on top, in the belief that it makes them appear 'tarty' or too highly sexed. Talking to one another about your needs and fears is one sure way to create the intimacy within a relationship that allows you to express your wishes and overcome your inhibitions.

At first I was really shocked when Alison told me what she wanted from me when it came to sex. Until then, I'd just assumed that what was great for me went for her too. I guess we just hadn't talked properly about sex, and there were things that I liked which she didn't. Once we found out where we both stood – what, I suppose, our hang-ups were – it was surprising how much it helped with ovecoming them. And now, one hang-up we don't have is being unable to talk about our sex life.

JAMES

Oral sex is considered by many people to be the most intimate form of loveplay. It is only within a truly trusting relationship that the full pleasures can be realized.

problem on your partner – if at the time it cannot be handled – is usually counter-productive; you can always come back to it at a future date. You could be surprised how much you agree about certain subjects, although you had never dared to express your true feelings before. Listen to your partner; put yourself in the other one's shoes and reflect back what you hear and observe. The aim is to try to understand what he or she is feeling. Along with this, try to become aware of the non-verbal communication that is going on by observing your partner's body language: your feedback can be even more helpful, and he or she will feel better understood. You will be amazed at how well you start to communicate with one another, even on very difficult subjects.

OVERCOMING INHIBITIONS

Overcoming your inhibitions about some aspect of your sex life – perhaps oral sex, different lovemaking positions, or something as simple as making love with the lights on – begins with sharing your concerns with a loving partner whom you trust intimately. It is essential to work through any problem together. Blackmail of the 'If you really loved me you would' variety can never work: it puts a severe strain on any relationship and results in little or no pleasure for both partners.

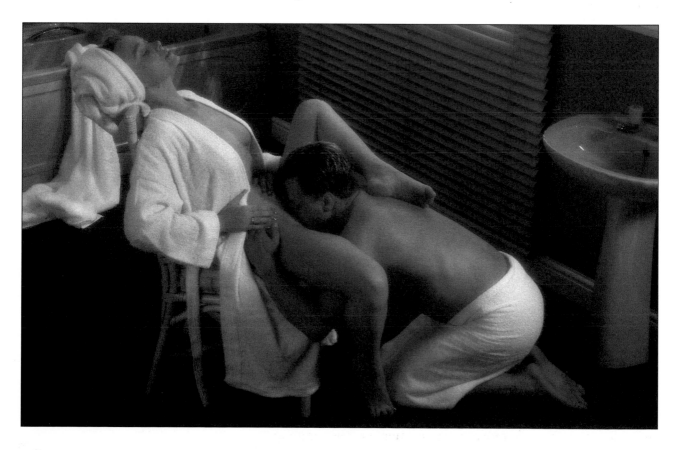

SENSUAL MASSAGE

I don't always feel at my best after a tiring day at work and often the last thing on my mind is sex. I'm too wound up for anything, really. But somehow Rob can always bring me round with massage. When he's massaging me, I can honestly say that all my tension is gradually released and my senses come back to life. I make sure that I enjoy every moment that he's stroking me – he's very good, you know. He never presses me into having sex with him, although after a massage I am more likely to want to make love. Massage for both of us is an important way of getting closer and staying close.

JEMILLA

𝒪ne of the best ways to discover one another's body is through massage. It is a satisfying form of loving behaviour in itself, and can be a sensuous prelude to lovemaking. In simple terms, massage is a structured way of touching each other. It is a beautiful way of getting closer and learning how to surrender.

Begin by lightly but firmly massaging your partner's back (1), keeping both hands in contact with the body on either side of the spine. Use oils or talcum powder to help your hands slide more smoothly. Always keep up a steady soothing rhythm over

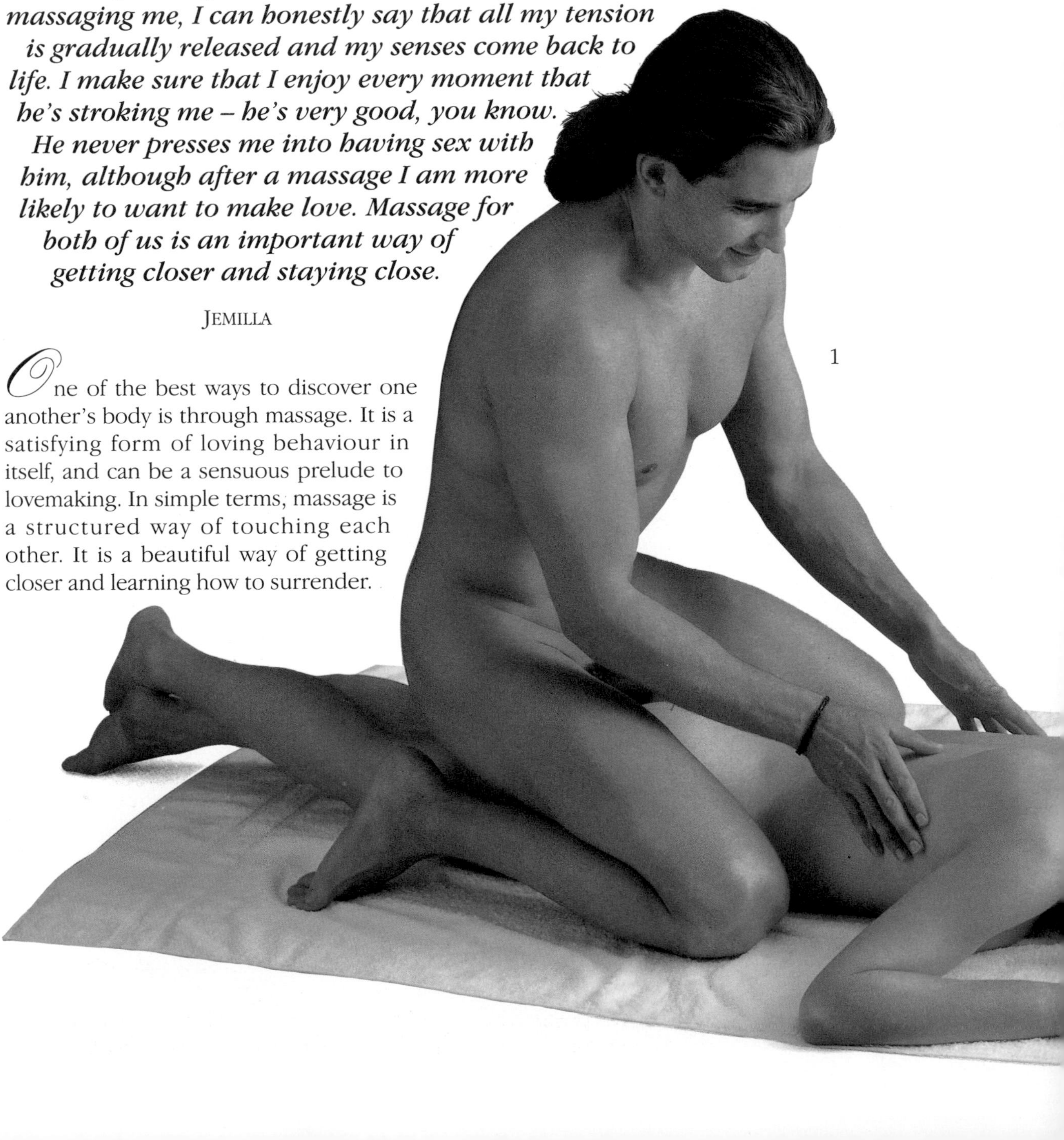

1

2

the back. Straddling your partner while you do this means he or she can feel the warmth from your inner thighs which can heighten pleasure. Next, move down to your partner's buttocks (2) where you can knead the fleshy parts quite firmly. The inside of the thighs is a highly erogenous area, so spend time softly stroking here to increase pleasure as your partner becomes even more relaxed. When you have worked all over your partner's body, start again using a different technique. Using your fingers lightly (3) to give feathery touches down the back can add quite different erotic sensations to a sensual massage. Experiment with different touches and discover what your partner likes best.

3

The basic aim is to produce relaxing and pleasurable sensations for the partner receiving, although naturally the giver also benefits from the other person's pleasure. Choose a place that is warm and comfortable, and a time when you will not be disturbed. Don't worry too much about technique, but rather learn from each other what feels best. Do not massage bony areas – stick to the fleshy parts and try to be gentle. Let your partner guide you by sounds of pleasure. Use soothing oils, or talcum powder, to make your hands slide smoothly over your partner's body, and try to maintain a rhythmic flow throughout.

Sensual massage, done with love and care, builds trust in a way almost nothing else can. You will become used to seeing your partner totally naked; you learn to trust him or her totally to handle you with reverence and respect; you learn to relax in someone else's company; and you can give and receive love and bodily pleasures without the pressure of having to have sexual intercourse.

TAKING IT FURTHER

If the mood is right, and one or other of you wants to take things further, it can be fun to make sensual massage more erotic. Instead of using your hands, try a feather, fur or even some melting ice. Try using your hair, your breasts, or your penis, to run over your partner's body. Again, always be guided by the receiver. Approach everything with your mind open, and your body relaxed, and you will be surprised to find out just which parts of your body can make you feel sexy, including those that had never occurred to you.

With practice and imagination, you will find that your instincts take you into realms of pleasure you had never dreamed of.

1

I go through phases. First I feel relaxed and rather dreamy as I let myself go completely, and then I start to feel really sexy. I'm almost desperate for Natalie to grab hold of my penis, but she just ignores it as she keeps massaging my front. It really winds me up and I just can't wait to make love to her.

SIMON

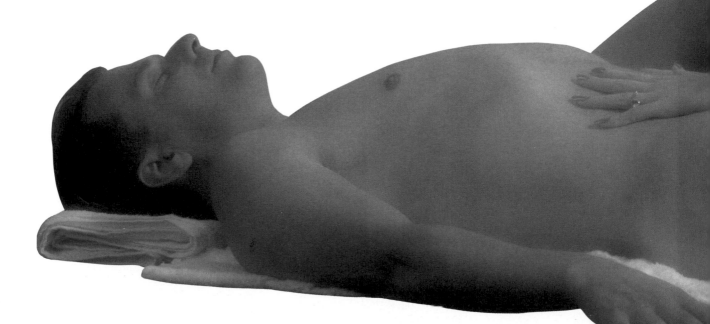

3

2

Try not to ignore any part of your lover's body. Massaging feet and toes, and hands and fingers, is wonderfully relaxing for the receiver, and can often create exceptional erotic feelings (1). When your partner is on his or her back, work along the chest, and thighs – but make sure that you ignore the genitals (2). And do not forget the neck and face; use firm but gentle touches here especially. Having massaged his or her entire body with your hands, use other parts of your body to give different sensations. The woman drawing her breasts and nipples gently across her lover's body can provide exquisite sensations (3). The man's penis on his partner can have similar pleasurable effects.

EXPLORING EACH OTHER

I guess I'd always been a bit frightened of getting too close to all of Sally's bits and pieces. I sort of knew what they were, and what they did, but one night, just as we were about to get on with our usual sex, I put my head down between her legs, and started kissing her. I don't know why I did it, but I felt like I wanted to get to know her properly. She told me where she liked being touched the most, and for the first time I started to lick and touch her in a way I hadn't done before. Now I've learned what she likes, this has added so much to our sex life for both of us.

STEVE

Having learned how to appreciate and touch one another naked, it is very helpful to get to know one another's genital geography and, eventually, patterns of arousal. In an ideal world this should happen at an early stage of a committed sexual relationship. But even after years of not getting this far, mutual exploration can bring real insights and benefits.

One day, when you are feeling really relaxed, try to overcome any shyness or inhibitions, and each take turns to examine one another's genitals in some detail. Do not hurry it. Take your time, and share with one another everything that you discover. Make sure you are comfortable, perhaps on the bed or the sofa, and that the room is warm. Make sure that no visitors are expected and that you will not be disturbed by the telephone. It is a good idea to shower or bathe first, so that you are both fragrant and fresh.

THE VULVA AND CLITORIS

The man should begin by simply looking at the outside of his partner's genitals – the vulva and the clitoris. What you can see are the outer lips. You may have to open these gently with your fingers to reveal the smaller, inner lips. These come together at the top to form a little hood which covers the tip of the clitoris. This is a highly sensitive organ: for most women stimulation of the clitoris is the best way to achieve orgasm.

What looks like an indentation, or even an obvious hole beneath

A man can begin getting to know his partner's genitals by looking at her vulva and clitoris.

1

2

3

After looking at your partner's vulva, part the outer lips gently to reveal the entrance to the vagina (1). Next, run your fingers up towards the clitoris to see how it is enclosed in its small hood (2). Just beneath the head of the clitoris is the entrance to the urinary tract. Now softly squeeze the outer lips between your fingers, to discover how they feel (3). Finally, insert a finger into the vagina and feel its walls, and then insert it further until you can feel the cervix – the neck of the womb (4). Massage the front wall of the vagina and try to find the swollen area of tissue that constitutes a woman's G-spot.

4

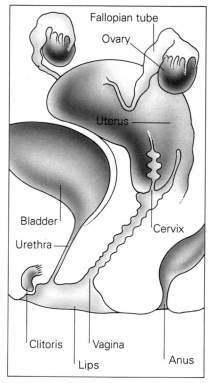

The anatomy of a woman's sexual organs (schematic).

the head of the clitoris is the opening to the urinary passage. Below this is the entrance to the vagina, and slightly further back, the anus. Around the opening of the vagina there are often small flaps of skin. These are the remains of the hymen – the membrane that sealed off the vaginal opening before your partner first had sex, or first used a tampon. In some women they may be very small and hard to see.

The next stage after looking is feeling. Go back up to her clitoris, and run your finger lightly over the body of the organ just above its head. It will probably feel like the end of a small pencil. Now touch the inner and outer lips and see what they feel like. Run your fingers along the two pairs of lips and then around the vaginal opening. Stroke the perineum – the bridge of tissue between the vagina and anus.

THE VAGINA

Now gently insert a finger into the vagina and feel its walls. You will find that they are wet and crinkly, especially along the front wall, up towards the woman's stomach. When a woman is unaroused, the walls of the vagina lie flat against each other, but lubricate when she is excited and move apart, and the space in the vagina increases.

THE WOMAN'S G-SPOT

On the front wall of the vagina there may be a sensitive area called the G-Spot, which gives pleasure when stroked. If stimulated for long enough, it can bring some women to orgasm. You may not be able to feel it unless the woman is aroused, as it swells up to form a distinct area only after lots of stimulation. Caressing the G-Spot can produce the sensation of wanting to pass water; this may come as a

1

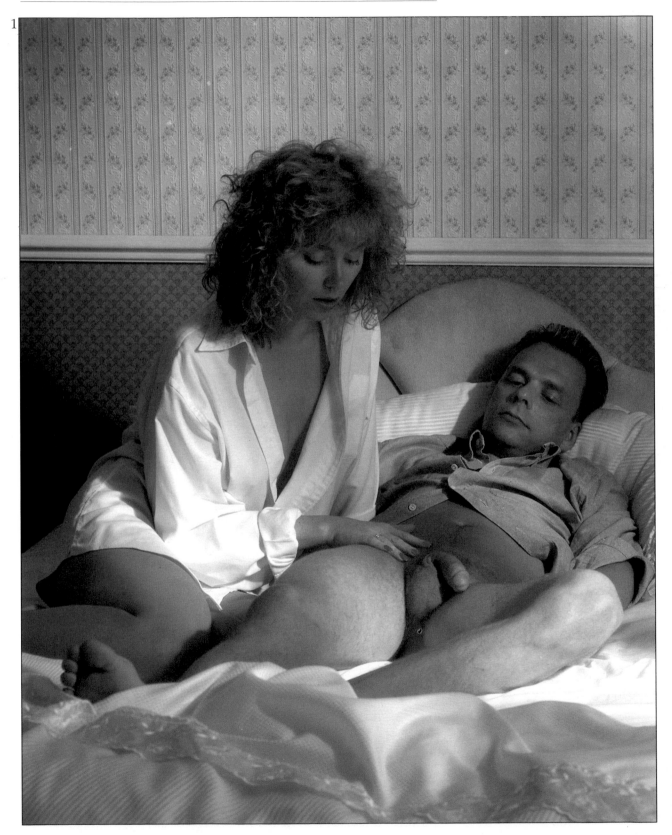

surprise the first time, but you will soon learn to distinguish the two different sensations.

Now push your finger in a little more, until you come to something that feels like the tip of your nose. This is the cervix, or neck of the womb; you might feel it with your penis when you penetrate very deeply.

THE PENIS

A man's genitals are easy to see, although many women have not taken the trouble to explore them in detail. The woman should start by looking at the penis itself because it is the most obvious part. Try to begin by looking at it when it is not erect, and then watch it change as your partner has an erection. When the penis is erect, gently pull back the foreskin – if the man has one – to reveal the glans or head. At its tip is the opening that lets out both urine and semen. Just underneath this is a little vertical ridge of skin, called the frenum. Most men say that this is their most arousing part.

THE TESTICLES

Next, turn your attention to his scrotum – the bag of skin that contains the testicles, or balls. You might be able to see the muscles in the scrotum contract under the skin, and the testicles move about. Now feel those: they are largely a mass of coiled tubes, containing sperm that are maturing in readiness for ejaculation. At the top of each ball is a hard core which you can be feel between your finger and thumb. This is the vas deferens – the tube which conveys

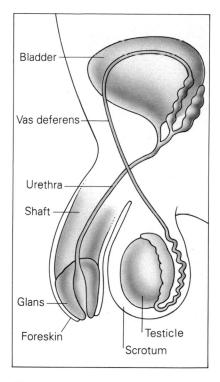

The anatomy of a man's sexual organs (schematic).

Paul's penis seemed so big when it was erect that at first I was a bit shy, and didn't know what to do with it. But one time when I was holding it in my mouth, I reached down and squeezed his balls too. He didn't have to tell me how much he really liked me doing this. Since then I've discovered more of what he likes, and our lovemaking has become much more fun.

SUZANNE

Begin by looking at the penis when it is limp (1) and then watch how it changes as it erects (2). Take notice of how the muscles of the scrotum – the bag of skin holding the testicles – tighten under the skin and the testicles move about.

2

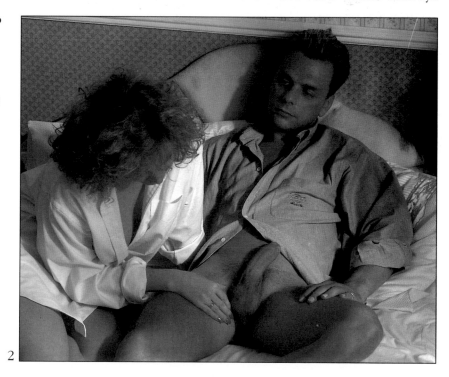

sperm to the glans of the penis at the moment of ejaculation.

Now move to the base of the penis and feel all around it. You will notice that the penis has a sort of 'root' that goes back towards the anus. Run your fingers along this, and around the anal area.

THE MAN'S G-SPOT

A man's G-Spot is located in his prostate gland, which can be reached by inserting a well-lubricated finger into his anus. The prostate feels like a firm mass of tissue about the size of a walnut, and is situated in the front wall of the rectum, or back passage. Gentle stimulation with the pad of the finger can create exquisite sensations and intense orgasms for a man. Some even say that it alters the whole orgasmic experience for them.

… AND AFTERWARDS

After these exploration sessions, take time, either then or later, to share what you have discovered. Was there anything new? Did anything surprise you? Remember, you can always go back and repeat all or some of the exercises another time. Being this open with each other shows real care, acceptance and interest in one another, and such intimate knowledge can make you feel very much closer.

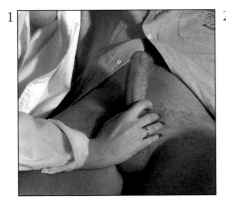

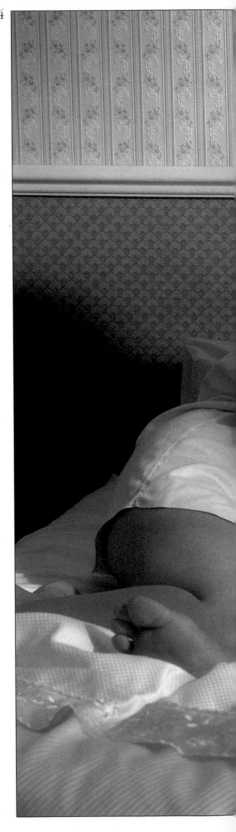

If the man has a foreskin, pull it back to reveal the glans (1). At the tip is a small hole that lets out both urine and semen . Run your thumb or finger around the ridge of the glans (2) and touch the vertical ridge of skin that runs from the shaft to the glans – the frenum (3). For many men this is the most sensitive part of the penis. Feel around the base of the penis to find the 'root' that runs back towards the anus (4), and around the anal area.

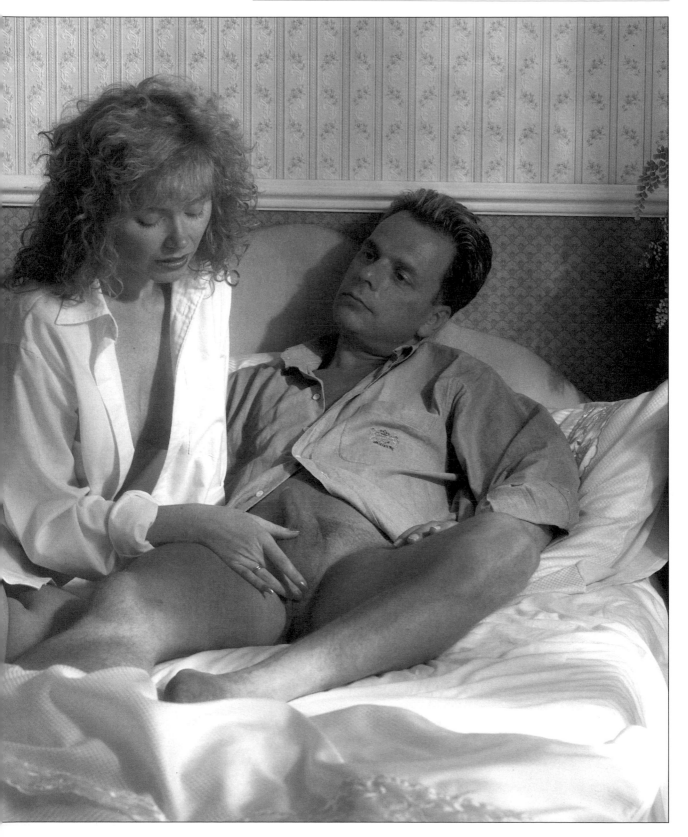

AROUSAL AND ORGASM

I won't forget the first time I had sex with Susie in a hurry. You could sense the electricity in the air between us. We'd been flirting all evening, and then suddenly she took me by surprise and kissed me on the neck in a way that sent a shiver right through me. I thought at first that I couldn't hold back a second longer. I was actually holding her close to me, and I could feel her nipples getting hard as I started to stroke her breasts. And then slowly she started to pull off my shirt, and push down my pants and trousers to show off my huge erection. By now I was bursting, but I managed to undress her in the same way. By the time we made love, we were both so aroused, it was the best orgasm I'd ever had.

MARK

Some time spent on foreplay is essential for both partners to be fully aroused. The man can usually respond with an erection very quickly, but the woman may need some time before her vagina is fully lubricated and ready to accept his penis comfortably. Orgasms are also more likely for the woman if she is fully aroused before penetration, and the man can benefit from bigger, firmer erections.

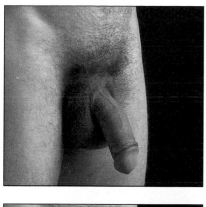

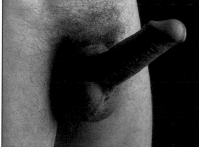

Words, sounds, smell and particularly sight trigger a man's erection. As he becomes aroused, blood flows into his penis and is trapped, causing the penis to grow thicker and longer. In its erect state, the penis naturally points upwards.

The first step on the journey through our sexual life is to accept our own body, care for it and respect it. This helps our personal sense of self-esteem and is a compliment to our partner. It shows that, by caring about and for ourselves, we care about them. A caring and sincere partner will always be more satisfying than one who just looks sexy.

Accepting ourselves also means acknowledging that we all have sexual needs; understanding our own, and our partner's, is important in building a long-term intimate relationship. Our first encounter with our sexual selves is usually during masturbation, an activity in which almost everyone indulges, if only from time to time. Masturbation can simply provide physical relief, but it is also an important milestone in understanding the changes that occur in our bodies when we feel sexy and move toward orgasm.

MAN'S AROUSAL

For a man, a highly effective trigger for sexual arousal is vision: bare flesh, revealing clothes, even red lipstick, can quickly arouse a man sexually. But we should not forget the power of the other senses. The sense of smell is stronger than many think, the sound of words of passion can be very arousing, as is touch on another's and our own erogenous zones.

The first obvious sign of a man's arousal is an erection: blood fills the tissue in the penis, causing it to stiffen and grow longer and thicker. As arousal increases so does the heart rate; breathing quickens and the nostrils flare. The skin of the scrotum thickens and retracts, and there is an increasing urge for further stimulation of the penis. When arousal reaches a certain point, ejaculation is imminent and a man cannot hold back. During orgasm, there is a rhythmic throbbing of the penis as semen is pumped out. The penis then becomes limp again, and it takes some time for a man to be ready for re-arousal.

After orgasm, many men feel tired, both physically and mentally, and tend to want to go to sleep. They are usually also resistant to any further sexual stimulation.

Other changes may occur in a man's body during sexual activity. About a quarter of men develop a 'sex flush' as their skin reddens across their chest, shoulders and arms. Others have nipple erections, as women do, and nipple stimulation can be another source of pleasure. Sweating during or after orgasm is quite common, but this is not directly related to the amount of physical effort that has gone into lovemaking.

WOMAN'S AROUSAL

The body changes in a woman when she is aroused are very similar to those in a man. However, the average woman usually takes longer to become aroused, remains aroused longer and – unlike a man – is capable of almost instant re-arousal. Also, women tend not to be as easily aroused by visual stimuli alone; they respond more to romance and intimacy and their partner's personality.

As excitement begins, a woman's nipples erect and her breasts swell. As more blood flows in, there may be a sex flush over her chest and neck, her lips redden and she begins to sweat slightly. The vagina becomes moist as a lubricating fluid is produced by its walls, to make penetration by the penis easier. The genitals begin to fill with blood which makes them swell and darken, especially around the inner lips. The outer lips also swell and open up, and the vagina becomes progressively more moist.

Stimulation of the clitoris makes it erect, although the response is not as quick as with penile erection. The clitoris can also become erect if other sexually sensitive parts of the body – such as the breasts or the vagina – are stimulated, but again the response is much slower than that in a man.

As sexual tension grows, the vagina balloons at its top end and the clitoris may seem to disappear as it retracts inside its hood. Orgasm itself occurs when there are intense contractions of the pelvic muscles and uterus. The woman's body may go into a sort of spasm, she may groan or cry out, and gasp or bite her lip as the sensations flood through her. In other women, though, the response may be less noticeable or dramatic.

After orgasm, it may take between 15 and 30 minutes for her body to return to normal, and again unlike men, most women welcome some form of loving behaviour during this period .

MULTIPLE ORGASMS

One difference between men's and women's sexuality is that women are more capable of having more than one orgasm during a single bout of lovemaking. While a man involuntarily returns quickly to the resting stage after orgasm, a woman may remain in a highly aroused state and, with further stimulation, some women can quite quickly reach orgasm as many times as they like.

SIMULTANEOUS ORGASMS

Many couples view simultaneous orgasm as the ideal goal of lovemaking. But while climaxing together can indeed be extremely pleasant, it should not become the aim of every lovemaking session. Enjoying each other's orgasms is the essence of a loving sexual relationship; if simultaneous orgasm becomes the sole purpose of lovemaking, this may lead to disappointment and even resentment. It can be worth trying for occasionally, however.

In most cases the man will have to slow down his orgasm and the woman speed hers up. Extended foreplay and high-level arousal for the woman is probably the first step. Choose a position in which she can control the rhythm, position and depth of pene-

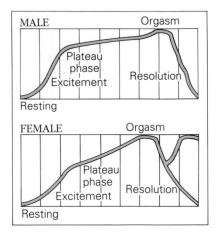

Human sexual response can be divided into five phases: resting, excitement, plateau, orgasm and resolution. During foreplay excitement increases in both men and women until they reach the plateau phase. Women generally take longer than men to reach this phase, which is why extended foreplay is so important. From the plateau phase, both men and women move towards orgasm. After orgasm, the man's resolution phase is short, perhaps only two or three minutes, until he returns to the unaroused resting phase. For the woman, resolution is slow and gradual, often lasting up to half an hour. Some women can delay this phase, and return to the plateau phase where they can be stimulated again to have another, multiple orgasm.

As a woman becomes aroused her outer lips swell and open up, revealing the inner lips which also swell and darken. The vagina begins to moisten. Her breasts swell, her nipples erect and the areola – the darker ring of skin around the nipple – grows smaller.

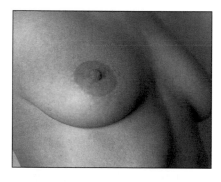

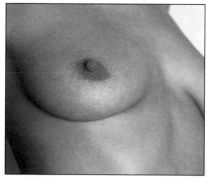

tration; any position that allows manual stimulation of her clitoris by either of you will help. Slowing down a man is slightly more difficult, but positions in which the man is lying on his back will tend to delay his response. You can also use the squeeze technique (see page 94).

One unfortunate side-effect of simultaneous orgasm is that even if both of you climax at the same time, it may not necessarily be pleasurable for either of you. A man trying to hold back his ejaculation can lose his timing and much of his pleasure, and the same is true for the woman who tries to hurry hers. It is important, however, for both partners to let each other know, by general body language, sounds or words, how close they are to climaxing. If trying for simultaneous orgasms ever detracts from you having pleasurable sex, it makes sense to stop.

UNDERSTANDING YOURSELF

Not every lovemaking session has to, nor indeed should, end in orgasm. Orgasm can be the natural outcome of lovemaking, but there are times when tiredness precludes it. For some women, too, achieving or enjoying orgasms can be more complicated, or subtle, than for men. With practice, and willingness to be open with your partner, it is possible to make real progress towards more reliable and more pleasurable orgasm.

Learn to relax with your own body; appreciate it, discover what feels nice about it, and let yourself go with your feelings. Discover your own body – both aroused and unaroused – through masturbation, and get to know what you like to do and where you would like to be touched by your partner. Watch your partner masturbate and learn what he or she likes best. Try to share your innermost feelings and experiences with your partner: you will come to realize how similar they are in many ways, and how you can learn and benefit from your differences. A couple who are intimate out of bed are invariably closer in bed.

It is easy to think that lovemaking centres on the genitals, and to miss out on the pleasures that can be derived from other parts of our own and our partner's body.

EXPLORE YOUR PARTNER

Explore your partner's body slowly and thoroughly. Try different forms of touch, such as kisses, nibbles or licking; stroke them lightly, then firmly, using your hair, breasts or penis to stimulate him or her. Take things slowly, and really begin to learn which parts of your partner's body gives them most pleasure. Spend time finding out what kind of stimulation is the most exciting. The important thing is always to let your partner know what pleases you – perhaps with a sigh of pleasure – and for your partner to feed back the enjoyment that comes from seeing you so excited.

EROGENOUS ZONES: HIM

*E*rogenous zones are those parts of the body that provide sexual excitement when touched or stroked; but excitement can be even more intense if these zones are kissed, licked or touched with the tongue. Although the genitals are the most sensitive areas of a man's or woman's body, many other areas can produce intense sexual sensations if stimulated properly. The best way to discover your partner's pleasure zones is through foreplay, and especially during sensual massage.

Generally, a man's body is less sensitive than a woman's, with only some areas of his body producing erotic feelings when stroked, caressed or kissed.

THE MALE ZONES

• *Any area of the face and neck, but in particular the lips, respond sensually to touch and kissing.*

• *Shoulders, back, chest and nipples will all provide pleasurable sensations if stroked. Sucking a man's nipples will often make them erect and become more sensitive to further stimulation.*

• *A man's buttocks can provide sensual feelings. There is no need to be gentle here – quite firm kneading provides the most pleasurable results.*

• *When massaged, his hands, fingertips and the soles of his feet can all provide erotic stimulation.*

EROGENOUS ZONES: HER

*I*n contrast, a woman's body is an erogenous zone as a whole, to a greater or lesser extent, and all of her skin is responsive to stimulation by hands, mouth or tongue.

THE FEMALE ZONES

• *Light touches on the cheeks, eyelids, eyebrows, forehead and along the hairline are enjoyed by most women. Kisses on the back of the neck and the earlobes, can have electric results.*

• *A woman's mouth, when stimulated by her lover's mouth or fingertips, can directly affect her entire body, and in particular her nipples and genitals.*

• *Arms, armpits and hands may all respond to sensual touching.*

• *Her back, hips and abdomen – especially around the navel – respond to light touches or kisses.*

• *Feet and legs produce pleasure for the woman when stroked; the insides of her thighs, and backs of her knees, also produce highly arousing sensations when they are kissed.*

• *A woman's breasts and nipples can be highly sensitive and for about half of women play a prime part in their sexual arousal. Stroking, kissing, sucking or gently nibbling can produce sensational effects.*

• *Buttocks are rich in nerves and can be stimulated by kneading, rubbing, patting or even gentle slapping.*

• *Stroking or kissing the perineum can be highly pleasurable.*

QUESTION TIME

Q I think our sex life is okay. We make love three or four times a week and both always climax. But my partner complains that she doesn't really enjoy our lovemaking that much – not like she used to when we first knew each other. Why?

A *You are right to be concerned and could take the responsibility of making things better. If the aim of your lovemaking is only geared to producing orgasms, over and above everything else, it is lacking the love and intimacy that makes sex special. It's time to make an effort outside the bedroom as well.*

The emotional side of a relationship is as important to many women as the physical side. Make a plan to go back to your original courtship behaviour, spend more time talking and have the occasional romantic evening together, either at home or out.

Q We've never had simultaneous orgasms, even though we've tried occasionally. Is there something that we are doing wrong?

A *Firstly, if trying for simultaneous orgasms gives neither of you any pleasure, then it is best to stop trying. It will happen from time to time*

anyway. Generally, if you do want to climax together, you will probably have to speed up the woman's response and slow down the man's. Extended foreplay using both hands and mouth to arouse the woman is usually necessary, while only little stimulation of the man's genitals should slow down his ejaculatory urge. Another way to slow down the man is to choose a woman-on-top position, or one that allows deep penetration so that the head of his penis receives less stimulation.

There are many people, however, who find non-synchronized orgasms far more rewarding. The fact that one partner puts his or her energy into pleasing the other, which is then reciprocated, emphasizes the giving and receiving that is the cornerstone of a loving relationship.

Q I've always been worried that my penis is rather small. Will this have any effect on my ability to provide orgasms for my partner?

A *No. Penis size is one of the big male hang-ups that leads to loss of self-confidence. The fact is that virtually every vagina will accommodate a penis of any size and be stimulated in the same way. Many women claim that the length of*

the penis has no effect whatsoever; its width is more important. The only problem for a man who imagines that he has a small penis is that he imagines that he has a small penis.

Q I have read that some women have more than one orgasm when they have sex, but I've never had more than one. Am I unusual?

A *Many women are able to have multiple orgasms by continued stimulation after the first orgasm. These women remain at the plateau phase of arousal, rather than entering the resolution phase, and from here can repeatedly reach orgasm.*

During intercourse a lot depends on her partner. He will need to hold back from his orgasm in order to maintain his erection, and therefore to prolong lovemaking.

A great many women report that the only way they can achieve multiple orgasms is through masturbation. Women who are capable of multiple orgasms do not have them every time they make love, nor do they necessarily want to. There is probably no reason whatsoever to stop you having as many orgasms as you like, provided that the stimulation is enough, and of the correct kind.

CHAPTER 2

KISSING AND CARESSING

How to use creative foreplay,

masturbation and oral sex as pleasures

in themselves and as important

preliminaries to more varied and

fulfilling lovemaking .

FOREPLAY

Before I met Malcolm, I can't really remember having any proper orgasms when I made love. It didn't bother me then, as I was still having a good time. Or so I thought. I suppose it's what you get used to, and what you don't know you don't miss. But from the very beginning with him, I knew that things were different. For a start, we spent a lot more time kissing and petting, which was something the other men I'd slept with weren't much interested in. All they wanted was to grab my breasts, dive straight in and have sex. Somehow Malcolm seemed to know when and where to touch me, and, for the first time, I felt sensations deep in my body that I hadn't felt before. He still stimulates me until I have this real ache for him to be inside me, and not long after he does finally slip himself into me, I have these incredibly powerful orgasms.

FIONA

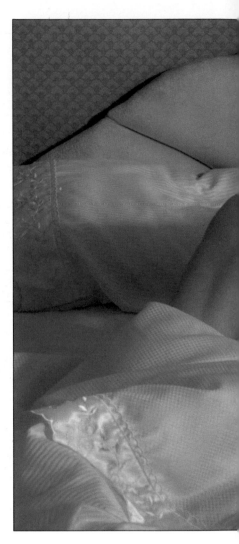

*T*he word foreplay is slightly misleading because it implies that it has to come before something else. But foreplay can be a delicious and rewarding pleasure in its own right, and there is no reason at all why sex should always involve intercourse. The art is to avoid the genital areas for as long as you can as you build up the excitement.

Because men are more easily aroused than women, they often rush too quickly into genital contact and penetration, ignoring the fact that a woman generally needs some time to become fully aroused. A sensitive man will try to control his impulses and take as long as necessary to arouse his partner, gradually building up her excitement before he moves on to stimulating her breasts and genitals. Extended foreplay is beneficial to both partners, the man achieving a firm erection and the woman becoming more moist, more receptive to intercourse and, as a result, more likely to reach orgasm easily.

Kissing, caressing and cuddling are all potent stimuli that trigger the release of sex hormones into the bloodstream. As these circulate, they act on a part of the brain which sends signals to create even more hormones.

KISSING

Whether you are with a new partner or in a long-standing relationship, do not forget the pleasures of foreplay. Building up the excitement gradually, by kissing and caressing each other, even before you undress completely, only serves to heighten the pleasures to come.

Foreplay and other pleasures can start outside the bedroom, of course. Our first physical encounter with a partner is usually kissing, a vastly enjoyable activity that is often overlooked – and underused once a relationship is established. In fact, when relationships go wrong, it is usually kissing that stops before intercourse does.

Try not to let your kisses be wet or slobbery and do not start with too much activity. Begin slowly and gently, with your lips relishing the contact. Do not ram your tongue instantly down your partner's throat. Tease a little by kissing other parts of your partner's face – the forehead, eyes, cheeks – as you draw your lips across. Let the passion grow slowly and delicately. Run your tongue around your partner's teeth and, as the excitement builds, push it further into the mouth. You can 'fence' with each other's tongue, or imitate the motions of sexual intercourse by thrusting your tongue in and out of one another's mouth.

Kissing, however, does not need to be restricted to the mouth.

Kisses on the earlobes, neck, throat and shoulders, or nibbling, or even gentle biting, can be highly erotic for both sexes. Try kissing and sucking fingers and toes and watching the response. Explore every part of your lover's body, even those you may think will not respond. For example, women like the backs of their knees and the inside of their thighs being kissed.

Many women's breasts are highly sensitive and should initially be stroked gently. Only when a woman is aroused will a firmer touch and kissing, sucking and gentle nibbling of her nipples be pleasurable. Many men, too, enjoy having their nipples caressed and kissed, in the same way as women do. Go all over your partner's body, first with kisses then with the tip of your tongue. Gently nibble and suck – or first wet and then blow on – particularly sensitive parts of your partner's body: the pleasures of giving can be as great as those of receiving. The genital kiss, perhaps the most intimate of all kisses, should be kept for later.

THE GENTLE TOUCH

Combine kissing with caressing and stroking your partner's body all over, first with a gentle touch and then building up the pressure as the excitement mounts. Avoid each other's genitals

Explore every part of your lover's body, concentrating on the areas that you know give the most pleasure, but avoid the genitals for as long as possible until you are both ready for intercourse. Use your own body, your hands, mouth and tongue to provide sensual feelings for your partner, and all the time be guided by watching one another's expressions and listening to the sounds of pleasure.

Do not always concentrate your caresses on the most obvious parts of the body. Massaging feet or hands, for example, can have a wonderfully relaxing and erotic effect. The art of successful lovemaking is to take as much time as you need, or wish.

I used to think that the quicker I could enter Maxine the better it was for me. But Maxine showed me that there was a whole range of sensations that I could enjoy. When she brushes my nipples with her lips or runs her fingers gently between my balls and anus I don't want the feelings to stop even though my erection seems to be bursting. Now, I like to hold back as long as I can when she fondles me, and I can really say that when I climax it is better than ever.

NEIL

and concentrate on other parts of your partner's body that you know can be particularly arousing. Both men and women, for example, enjoy having their buttocks stroked, squeezed or kneaded, and even gently smacked. A finger run lightly around the anal area can also create exquisite sensations.

Use all of your body to tease and to rub up against your partner. The woman can use her breasts, nipples or hair to run over the man's body, to create sensations quite unlike those given by hands and fingers. He can use his penis and scrotum in exactly the same way, pleasuring her by drawing them gently across the most sensitive parts of her body.

All men enjoy having their penis held and most enjoy having their testicles held, or even gently squeezed; but it is generally best for a woman to avoid touching the man's genitals for too long before she is really ready for penetration. This is because extensive stimulation of this kind is often enough to bring a man to climax before intercourse.

For a woman, excessive genital caresses before she is aroused may be irritating rather than exciting. The first touch should be gentle, with her partner building up the pressure and movement as she nears orgasm.

UNDRESSING

Undressing in a provocative way can be an exciting part of foreplay. Revealing their body, or their partner's body, in a tantalizing way can be a turn on for both men and women. But it must be said that most men respond much quicker to visual stimuli, and that a hint of nudity will often have a stronger effect than complete nakedness Slowly removing clothes that emphasize breasts and buttocks is always a turn on for a man.

If a woman is confident enough to strip for her lover, this can be highly erotic for him as he can take the passive role in the proceedings for a while. And for men who feel that they have to be the initiators of lovemaking this will be highly arousing.

Try undressing each other, also, so each of you can show off your bodies in a passive way. Remember that you do not have to remove all your clothes to make love, and that both men and women can find it highly enjoyable if their partner retains an undergarment.

EROTIC MATERIALS

It can be fun occasionally to experiment with different sensations of touch during foreplay. Use different materials, for example fur or feathers, to draw across each other's bodies. Ice can also have an electric effect when run across the skin, and even the genitals. But make sure that the ice is not straight from the freezer as it can stick to the skin and burn.

MASTURBATION

When we first started living together and then got married, I just never would have masturbated. I would have felt it was a kind of betrayal, you know. Then, he went on this training course to do with work, and he was away for a week and one morning, well it just sort of happened. Then I thought, why not? It's such a release and there's no one else involved. Anyway, I usually fantasize about him so it's a kind of compliment. He's now got promotion and has to travel quite a lot and I still masturbate when he's away. But now I find that I also do it when he's here. It doesn't mean that I enjoy sex with him any less or that I prefer masturbation. Actually, sometimes the better sex is with him the more I want to bring myself off, do you see that? It's just totally different from anything we do together – unless, of course, I'm doing it in front of him. He likes me to do that too sometimes. The way I see it, it's an extension of my sex life with him.

NICOLA

*C*ontrary to what many want to believe, masturbation is not something that stops when two people become involved in a loving sexual relationship. Research shows that nearly all men, and most women, continue to masturbate throughout their active sexual lives. It need not be a solitary activity, implying sexual frustration, but a continuing source of self-pleasure, development and a safe release.

WATCHING EACH OTHER

Mutual masturbation is an ideal way to learn how to pleasure each other as part of extended foreplay. The only way to really learn how best to masturbate your partner is to watch how she or he masturbates. Watching and noting the other's reactions, how hands and fingers are used, which areas appear to be more sensitive, noting breathing and sounds of pleasure can be really useful. Remember to discuss what you have learned while you kiss and cuddle afterwards.

Of course, many people prefer to tell, rather than show, their

When women masturbate they use stimuli that change as they become more excited.

Note the change of position of your partner's hand as she brings herself to climax – how she stimulates her outer lips (1), if and when she inserts a finger (2) or the pressure and rhythm she uses on her clitoris (3).

1

2

3

partner what gives them more pleasure. But although you may find it difficult or embarrassing at first, you will find the benefits are definitely rewarding. Using what you learn to please each other, you can aim to masturbate your partner as well as they do themselves, if not better.

THE WOMAN

Women often start masturbating slowly, and build up the movement and pressure gradually. Watch her initial speed and rhythm, how many fingers she uses, what parts of her body she stimulates most. Women, unlike men, do not always re-create the actions of intercourse, or of a penis thrusting in and out; they use a pattern of stimuli, and not always aimed directly at producing an orgasm. Many women concentrate on stimulating the clitoris alone; some women stimulate only the vaginal lips, and insert one finger or maybe more.

Observe the speed, pressures and rhythms as she reaches her arousal plateau: many women at this stage prefer a steady rhythm. This is particularly important, as women often say that men do not maintain the right rhythm and pressure at the crucial time.

The main thing to learn is that everyone has their preferences, and that your partner is unique. Movements can be circular or up or down, pressure can be hard or soft or a combination of the two at different times. Watch where she puts her other hand if she is not using both. Does she caress her breasts, or thighs? Many women enjoy more than just the direct stimulation of the genital area. By watching their partner's actions and getting further guidance, most men can learn the art of masturbating a woman to the mutual satisfaction of both.

THE MAN

Generally, most men tend to masturbate in the same way. Their aim in masturbating is to re-create the movements of intercourse so they encircle the penis with one hand and pump up and down. The rim of the penis and the frenum are stimulated by the thumb and index finger. How hard a man grips is a matter of personal preference. As his orgasm approaches his hand movements become more rapid, but as he ejaculates the pumping action slows down considerably or even stops, as the head of the penis is very sensitive at this stage, and over-vigorous stimulation can be painful.

The main things to look for as you watch the man masturbate are the position of his hand and the location of his fingers on his penis. Note the type of strokes he makes. Are they long or short, slow or jerky? Look out for changes in his body as he nears orgasm. Do his penis, scrotum and testicles undergo any changes? Learn to recognize the appearance of the pre-ejaculatory fluid – a lubricant which precedes the ejaculation of semen; it will tell you how aroused he is. What does he do with his other hand at the moment of ejaculation? Does he stimulate other parts of his body such as his anus, scrotum or nipples? Most importantly, note when he stops stimulating himself and any changes that occur as he relaxes.

PLEASURING EACH OTHER

After a few sessions of watching each other masturbate, you will have learned a lot. Choose a comfortable position for your partner – one in which you will not tire too easily. It makes sense, if you are right-handed, to be on your partner's right, for example.

The main thing for the woman to remember is to hold the shaft of the penis firmly, just below the head. Remember, a loose grip can be more frustrating than enjoyable. For a woman there is a variety of ways to hold the penis: she can use the finger and thumb 'ring' technique, or grasp it with the whole hand. She can also roll the penis between her hands or against her thigh like dough. Whatever you do, make sure that your hand does not get tired. Change hands if it does. Ask your partner what feels good and try to replicate what you have learned from watching him masturbate.

For more exotic masturbation, try using both hands so the entire penis is encased, or wrapping your hair around his penis. Try using fur or feathers. Perhaps the most delicious form of

When the man begins to masturbate, his partner should note how he holds his penis and what he does with his other hand as he becomes more excited. As he nears orgasm, look for the changes in the speed, rhythm and grip of his hands. Watch the expression on his face so you can know when he is about to climax.

I remember in the early stages of our relationship Alan once said , 'You're not doing it right' and I just said, 'Well do it yourself' – and he did! I was shocked at first, even a little hurt, but then it was just fascinating to watch. The whole way he handled it was different – I suppose I found out quite a lot. Then one time we were just about to make love and I asked him if he'd like to see me touch myself. When he said yes, I was suddenly unsure but then began to relax when I saw how much it turned him on.

SUE

When you have learned how your partner masturbates, it is time to take turns to masturbate each other. Using what you have learned, the aim is to try to masturbate your partner as well as they do themselves – and maybe even better – to give as much pleasure as possible.

Hanna's made herself have an orgasm in front of me a couple of times now, and I've learned so much. I've learned how to tickle her clitoris and how she likes to push down on her pubis. I also realized that I was rubbing too hard and too fast. So now when I touch her slowly and softly, she not only enjoys it more, but I relax knowing that I'm doing the right thing.

IAN

masturbation for a man is to have his penis gripped between your breasts.

The man masturbating a woman must remember that the clitoris is a very delicate organ and should be treated gently, especially at first. His fingers should be lubricated with saliva, or vaginal fluid, as the whole genital area is sensitive to friction. Be guided by your partner, but generally a woman prefers fairly gentle pressure at first, only building up as she nears orgasm. Stimulation of the clitoris can be direct or indirect, but do not apply direct pressure unless your partner enjoys it.

Start by putting your whole hand over the vulva and making either circular or vibrating movements. Be guided by what she likes best. As she becomes more aroused, try inserting a finger into her vagina and moving it slowly in and out as you stimulate her clitoris. Don't be afraid to let her guide your hand and fingers to exactly the spot she likes best. And all the while do not forget to stimulate her breasts and other parts of her body. When she reaches orgasm

When you have learned how to masturbate each other well, it is time to try masturbating each other at the same time.

For a man, perhaps the most delicious form of masturbation is to have his penis gripped between the woman's breasts.

do not stop stimulating her clitoris: some women need continued clitoral excitement during orgasm. Ask her what is best.

When both of you are confident that you can masturbate one another well, try masturbating each other at the same time. Choose a position in which you are both comfortable, and take it in turns to bring each other to orgasm or, with a little practice, perhaps to simultaneous orgasms.

Try to make oral sex the end point of a series of kisses that you have placed all over your partner's body. For the woman who is giving, run your tongue over the head of the man's penis, pushing it into the small slit at the tip (1). Next, swirl your tongue around the rim of the head and vibrate it against the frenum (2).

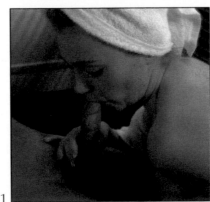

1

2

ORAL SEX

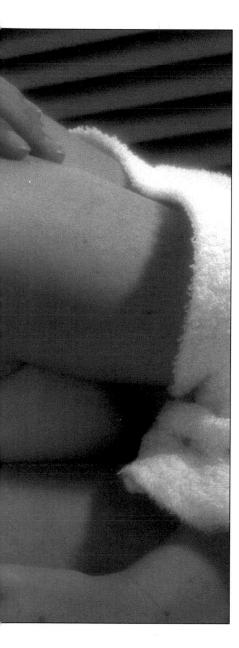

Neither of us wanted to rush into having oral sex, but I think that's mainly because we were both shy. Sally seemed worried about me ejaculating in her mouth, and that I would dislike her taste, or her smell. Well, we both talked about it for a while, and decided that the best thing to do was to take it gradually, until it felt right to try it. Once she had tasted my semen, she said it wasn't as bad as she had imagined, which was a relief. And far from disliking her taste, not only do I love it, but I have found one of the greatest sensations of all, which is when she has her vaginal spasms wrapped around my tongue.

PETER

Licking or sucking your partner's genitals is, in most peoples' minds, the most intimate thing you can do together in a sexual relationship. The very act demonstrates an enormous amount of trust, not only because it can be painful for either partner if not done carefully, but also because it shows an acceptance of each other that is more far-reaching than any other type of lovemaking. For many couples, oral sex is simply an extension of sensual foreplay and a prelude to intercourse, while for others, even if only from time to time, it is the way to orgasm.

Barriers to enjoying oral sex are nearly always in the mind. Either partner may worry about their genital odour and taste but this can be overcome by attention to hygiene and daily bathing or showering. Taking a bath together and washing each other as part of foreplay should allay any fears. In fact nearly all men find the taste of the slightly acid vaginal juices enjoyable and some find it one of the greatest taste bud sensations.

For many a woman the fear of her partner ejaculating in her mouth can cause concern. Always agree beforehand if this is unacceptable. The man should signal when he feels the urge to climax, and then withdraw if that is what has been agreed. His partner can continue to masturbate him to orgasm or move on to intercourse. A woman who is unsure about swallowing semen can always begin by spitting it out, until she gets used to the taste and volume of her lover's ejaculation. She may also worry about choking if the penis is thrust too deeply into her mouth. This can be overcome, if she controls how much of the penis she takes into her mouth by encir-

Many men enjoy having their testicles sucked and kissed, especially if the woman masturbates them at the same time (1). When the woman is ready, she can take the head of the penis into her mouth (2), moving it up and down firmly and in a steady rhythm to bring the man to orgasm. Her partner can gently hold the woman's head to slow down or speed up the rhythm.

A pleasurable variation for oral sex is if the man stands and the woman kneels in front of him as she takes his penis into her mouth. The important thing to remember is to try to keep the penis pointing upwards, otherwise it can be painful for the man.

cling the shaft of the penis with her hand. And a man should not thrust violently, especially when he reaches the point when he is about to climax.

For a man, having his penis sucked or licked is the ultimate in eroticism and probably the most powerful sexual stimulus that he can receive. To him the mouth feels like a 'different' vagina, providing an extra sensation from his partner's tongue stimulating the sensitive parts of his penis's head. For a woman, having her vaginal area, and particularly her clitoris, kissed, licked or sucked can be equally exciting. Although the tongue cannot penetrate the vagina very deeply it is capable of more varied stimulation than a man's fingers or penis, and has a much softer, wetter feel. By using his tongue and lips together he can provide highly arousing sensations to the clitoral and vaginal area at the same time.

Remember that teeth are sharp and the genitals somewhat sensitive, so try to cover your teeth with your lips and be careful not to bite if you become very excited. Also, never blow into your lover's genitals. This can be dangerous for both partners as it can force air into the bloodstream with serious consequences.

FROM HER TO HIM

Choose a relaxing and comfortable position at first; your partner lying down on his back or his side is probably the best. For variations, he can stand while you kneel in front of him, or he can sit in a chair or on the edge of the bed. Whatever position you choose, try to keep his penis pointing upwards as it can be painful for him

1 if you pull it down too far when you are sucking.

Begin by kissing other parts of your lover's body before moving on to his genitals. Kiss and lick the inside of his thighs, and even his scrotum which is also very sensitive. Tease him slightly while gently masturbating him, then gradually move down towards his penis. Start to kiss and lick it, then hold the shaft firmly and run your tongue across the head, pressing your tongue into the hole. Next, run your tongue around the ridge between the head and the shaft of the penis and flick your tongue against the frenum. Try licking the length of the shaft of the penis as if it were an ice lolly, and trip your tongue over the ridge. Experiment with any combination of these movements until you are ready to take his penis into your mouth.

Keep your teeth covered with your lips and gently take the glans into your mouth. There is a whole range of sensations that you can now create for your partner. Sucking, using your tongue on the shaft or head, or pushing his penis in and out of your mouth will all create different pleasurable effects. As you become more confident about oral sex you can experiment with other movements and sensations.

In the 'from him to her' situation described on page 52, the woman can sit on a chair, or on the edge of the bed, so that her partner has better access to every part of her genitals (1). He can easily reach her clitoris and can insert his tongue into the entrance of her vagina to mimic the motion of intercourse (2).

2

Another exciting variation of 'from him to her' is for the woman to sit over her partner's face while he uses his tongue and lips to stimulate her. One advantage is that the woman has a certain amount of control and can direct the man's tongue to where she likes it best.

Use your hands to stimulate other sensitive parts of his body, such as his nipples and buttocks, while you are sucking him to build up the excitement. A finger run lightly around his anal area, or inserted shallowly into his lubricated anus can create delicious orgasms for him.

To bring your partner to orgasm, move your mouth up and down his penis in a steady rhythm, making sure that you keep a firm pressure. Let him guide you by placing his hands on your head so he can slow you down or speed you up as he feels the need. As your speed increases he will reach the brink of orgasm, so hold the shaft with one hand if you do not want him to thrust too deeply, and help him to withdraw if you do not want him to ejaculate in your mouth.

FROM HIM TO HER

When you have oral sex with a woman, take things gradually. Try to make it the end point of a blanket of kisses that you have laid all over her body. Probably the best position is for the woman to lie on her back, with her legs apart and her hips slightly raised on a pillow, so that the man can easily reach every part of her genitals.

The inside of a woman's thighs is particulary sensitive, so begin by kissing and gently licking there as a hint of what is to come. Kiss her pubis, first gently then more firmly, before you run your tongue along the outer lips. Part them gently with your tongue, gradually running it up towards her clitoris. She may like you to part her lips with your fingers and thrust your tongue in and out of her vagina – to simulate the movements of your penis when you make love. All sorts of variations are possible. Try whirling your tongue around the entrance to her vagina, using a firm

The celebrated '69' position is often regarded as the ultimate in oral sex. It does, however, need a certain amount of practice to make it satisfactory for both partners. In this position you can either take it in turns to climax, or try for simultaneous orgasms. But be careful not to bite your partner's genitals in the ecstasy of climaxing.

I'm sure a lot of people worry about oral sex. It's just that you really have to know someone well and really care about them if you are going to do it. But when you do there's nothing to beat it. It is probably one of the great pleasures in life. It is wonderfully erotic and also such a commitment to each other that everything you do sexually afterwards is just that much more special.

SHIRLEY

lower lip to rub her pubis, gently tugging at her vaginal lips with your mouth, sucking her clitoris as it erects. After some sessions of oral sex, and a few experiments, the man should learn what his partner likes best.

Many women need direct stimulation of their clitoris to have an orgasm. Be firm but gentle, as the clitoris is sensitive and can become very tender. Vibrating your tongue against the clitoris, keeping a steady but accelerating rhythm, is the best way to bring your partner to orgasm. But be guided by her. As she nears her climax, she may make pelvic movements to direct the speed and pressure that she wants, so try to keep your head steady and let her push against you. During all this time caress her body, particularly her breasts and buttocks, to give her maximum pleasure.

There are many variations to try. A rear-entry approach can be be difficult at first for the man to reach the clitoris, but this can be overcome with practice. A big turn on for many couples is for the woman to sit over the man's mouth and direct her vagina and clitoris onto his tongue. The feeling of the woman being in charge can be extremely exciting.

FOR BOTH

Many people believe that the ultimate in oral sex is the position known as '69' where you can both give and receive simultaneously. Whether the man or the woman is on top, or you are side by side, this position can be extremely exciting and arousing during lovemaking. However, it does have drawbacks. Some men say that they find it difficult to stimulate their partner properly from this angle. It is also essential to keep a degree of control – because in letting go when you climax you may inadvertently bite your partner – which could diminish the pleasure of their and your own orgasm.

As with all forms of lovemaking, each individual and couple will discover what suits them best over a period of time. There is never a right or wrong way to do it.

QUESTION TIME

Q When my lover masturbates me before we have intercourse he makes it feel good to begin with, but then somehow it all goes wrong and I lose the feeling of wanting to climax. Is there anything I can do?

A *One thing you can do is to show him exactly how you masturbate yourself to orgasm, the way you change the pressure and rhythm of your hand, and the parts of your genitals that you stimulate as your arousal increases. For men, masturbation mimics the motions of intercourse, while in women there is a whole pattern of stimuli that are used.*

It can be difficult for men to realize this unless they are helped by their partner. Most men are only too pleased to be shown how to give their partner maximum pleasure, so do not be afraid to show him how to masturbate you in the way you like best.

Q I want to give my partner oral sex but I am really worried about him ejaculating in my mouth. What can I do?

A *The first thing to do is to agree between yourselves that he will not ejaculate in your mouth. He should signal to you when he is about to climax and then you can remove his penis from your mouth. The*

most common fears for women are that the volume of semen will be too much to swallow, and what it will taste like. The average man ejaculates about 10 cc, or the volume of a sugar cube, and to put your mind at rest it is worthwhile masturbating him to see exactly how much there is.

You can then try tasting it – it will be a rather bland, slightly salty taste which some women liken to oysters. If you do not want to swallow the semen you can take it into your mouth and then discretely spit it out. The important thing is to talk to your partner about how you feel, and then decide together on how you are going to proceed.

Q We have a really active sex life, but sometimes I still masturbate even when my partner is around. Am I unusual?

A *Most men, and many women, continue to masturbate throughout their active sexual lives, even when in a permanent relationship. Very often, the better the sex life the more people masturbate, as there is a constant high level of sexual arousal.*

As many people fantasize about their partner when they masturbate, it only helps to strengthen the relationship.

Another benefit is that the

release of orgasm during masturbation can take the pressure off needing, or wanting, to have intercourse at every opportunity. It also gives you more time to talk and spend more time to show each other loving behaviour before you jump into bed together – all things that create the intimacy that sustains a truly loving relationship.

Q When my boyfriend kisses me I just feel so sexy. My nipples erect and my vagina goes wet almost immediately. I'm worried that I'm oversexed if that's all it takes to get me going.

A *For both men and women – but particularly women – the mouth and lips are highly erogenous zones as they are full of sensitive nerve endings. For a woman, a particularly sensitive and erotic kiss can instigate sensual responses throughout her entire body. Unfortunately, too many men forget this and try to caress a woman's breasts and genitals as soon as they think it is possible. Kissing, holding hands, caressing almost any part of the body that is not obviously associated with sex, can show loving and caring in a far more intimate way and can often trigger much stronger responses.*

CHAPTER 3

MAKING LOVE

How to improve your lovemaking to

create greater pleasure for one another

with a guide to the various positions

and how they can increase sensual

enjoyment for both.

BETTER LOVEMAKING

When we first started to have sex I think we tried every position we could think of in those first few months. After a while, you get to know which ones suit you both, which give the most pleasure and stimulation. For instance, I could tell what Phil liked best from his face, or by the way his body reacted to certain things. His favourite is the doggie position which gives very deep penetration. It also allows him to reach around my breasts and clitoris. My favourite is being on top so that I can set the pace and rhythm, in fact be completely in charge, and, more important, to see his response.

SABRINA

While masturbation and oral sex are satisfying forms of sexual activity in themselves – whether they are used to prolong love-play or end in orgasm – penetrative sex is still seen as the culmination of sexual activity by most people.

Most couples, in the early stage of their relationship, experiment with many different positions and eventually settle down to a few favourite ones. Some positions may be used only occasionally, depending on how a couple feel emotionally and physically. Other couples will use several positions during one lovemaking session. A particular position may be enormously exciting for one partner but not for the other, and each may need to be in a different position to reach orgasm. Nobody becomes an expert overnight, and it usually takes a few months of pleasurable experimentation before you discover what you both like best.

PENETRATION

There are reasons why different positions create different sensations. The prime one is the angle at which the penis enters the vagina and the depth to which it penetrates. Generally, when a woman has her legs straight, penetration is at its shallowest, and when they are drawn back, deepest. By altering the angle of her legs, a woman can make the man's penis come into contact with almost anywhere within her pelvis. Very deep penetration can be achieved if the woman is on all fours, in a 'doggie' position, and this also allows the penis to stimulate the area around her G-spot.

Sex at its best involves quite a lot of movement, and certain posi-

Recent research has found that by far the best way to stimulate the clitoris during intercourse is to adopt a position in which the man rides high, with his pelvis over-riding the woman's.

The shaft of his penis can now rub on her pubic bone. He rests the full weight of his body on his partner, his torso pushing forward towards her head and shoulders. The woman wraps her legs around his thighs, with her ankles resting on his calves.

Once in this position, movement is almost entirely between the pelvic areas of both partners. At this point it is best to establish a rhythm in which the woman leads the upward stroke by forcing the man's pelvis backwards. He allows this to happen while applying counter pressure to her clitoral area. As her pelvis moves forwards and upwards, his penis is engulfed more deeply.

In the downward stroke the movements are reversed, the man's pelvis pushing the woman's backwards and downwards. She now tries to keep her clitoris in contact by pressing it against his penis. This kind of rocking movement ensures that the penis is kept in close contact with the clitoris at all times. Maintaining a slow and steady rhythm, without feeling any urgency to reach for orgasm, can produce exquisite climaxes for both. Indeed, many couples claim that orgasms resulting from this technique are superior to any other. Simultaneous orgasms are more common, too.

tions are preferable depending on who wants to move. A man who wants to have an orgasm during intercourse will need to experience penile movement. Most men enjoy thrusting movements of different speeds and depths, and they tend to thrust deeply once the inevitability of orgasm is upon them. All men are different, of course – some enjoy short, jerky thrusts, others long, slow ones – but any man will try to reproduce the movements that he creates during masturbation.

WHAT WOMEN LIKE

Women enjoy the sensation of the thrusting movements of the penis, and a man can create much pleasure for his partner if he takes his time before going for his own orgasm. Most women say that they prefer slow penetration and a slow lingering rhythm as the pleasure mounts towards orgasm, and a penis that thrusts for too long or too deeply can simply be painful.

In a lovemaking position in which he can move well, the man can create all kinds of pleasurable sensations for his partner. Try withdrawing slowly right to the opening of the vagina and tugging at her inner lips with the head of the penis. Tease her with the tip of your penis with shallow thrusts. Alternate between shallow and deep thrusts, or move your hips to change the angle at which you penetrate and thrust from left and right. There are endless combinations to try.

Woman-on-top positions allow her to take control of the angle, speed and depth of penetration. Rear-entry positions have the advantage of allowing both partners to move freely. If you find a position in which you both have a degree of freedom of movement, try sharing the thrusting movements. The man can withdraw a little and his partner push against his penis and then withdraw a little herself. These movements can be continued until orgasm is reached.

A woman could also try contracting the vaginal opening and deep pelvic muscles around her partner's penis as it moves inwards, and relax them as it moves outwards. This technique is highly stimulating for both partners, and can quickly bring a man to orgasm. The man, meanwhile, could try 'twitching' his penis to reciprocate the action.

CLITORAL STIMULATION

For women to climax there usually needs to be stimulation of the clitoris. During intercourse the clitoris is stimulated indirectly by the penis as it moves in and out of the vagina: the thrusting movement pulls on the inner lips which are attached to the hood of the clitoris. Many women, however, experience little or no clitoral stimulation from penile thrusting alone and need more direct caresses, perhaps with a hand.

Different lovemaking positions alter the angle at which the penis enters the vagina and the depth to which it penetrates. By trying different positions, almost every part of the vagina can be stimulated, with corresponding different sensations for the man's penis as well.

It's true what they say – size doesn't matter, it's what he does with it. John's really great the way he teases me with his penis. He's always changing the way he thrusts, deep or shallow, or he pushes into me sideways a little or swirls it round inside me. But he's always steady, building me up slowly but surely and I get these incredible feelings even before I climax.

MIRANDA

FIRST-TIME SEX

*S*ex with a partner for the first time is, unfortunately, not always the magical moment that we hoped for. So if you are disappointed do not be surprised. Making love is like most things in life: practice improves both performance and satisfaction. Knowing your partner's needs and wishes – and for that matter your own as well – comes only with time and willingness on the part of the couple to communicate to each other their feelings and sexual needs.

If we look at the circumstances of most people's first sexual experience, or the first time we make love with any new partner, there are many reasons why things do not work out as we hope.

When you have sex for the first time, or with a new partner for the first time, the ideal location is somewhere where you can be comfortable and remain undisturbed. Extended foreplay is essential to ensure that the woman is fully aroused and well lubricated before you attempt penetration. Resist the temptation to jump into bed straightaway.

LOVE, LUST OR CURIOSITY?

The reasons for having sex with someone are incredibly varied, and they have an influence on your feelings of joy or your disappointments. For a couple who have known each other for some time, and for whom making love is a way of cementing a long term relationship they both want, it can be an ecstatic experience. Throughout their courtship they will have learned about each other's likes and dislikes. By kissing, cuddling, touching and perhaps even masturbating each other, they will have built up a sense of intimacy, and a loving behaviour in which both are relaxed and happy to give and receive sensual pleasures. For this kind of loving couple, penetrative sex is just a milestone on their sexual journey together, rather than the culmination of it.

There are, however, some couples who have met only a few hours before they are in bed together. Perhaps the release of orgasm is all they think they need at the time, but the feelings afterwards are often of guilt and dissatisfaction, which can leave both partners feeling unhappy.

Clinical experience shows that in one-night stands, or even in short term relationships, men often have problems of both arousal and performance. In such a case it may be helpful for the woman to be sensitive, and to show through her behaviour that she still cares for the man. Spend time arousing him, using your hands and masturbating him gently until he has a firm erection. Using your mouth on his penis is nearly always a surefire way of arousing or re-arousing a man – and it may result in a satisfying experience for you too. If, however, everything fails, then perhaps try again another day. Or masturbate yourself to orgasm and tell him that being close to him turns you on.

For a man to climax too quickly, on the other hand, is also a great drawback, and a source of disappointment for the woman. Premature ejaculation is common in inexperienced, and particularly young, men and often occurs during first-time sex. If this happens, remember that men need time after orgasm before they can be re-aroused.

WRONG TIME, WRONG PLACE

First-time sex often takes place in locations in which neither partner can relax properly. This is especially true of young couples who perhaps still live with their parents, and can never find the privacy they need. Making love in the back of a car, or any other semi-public place, neither gives you the time nor the comfort to enjoy sex in a full way – although of course 'quickies' can have their own erotic appeal.

Try to find a place and a time when you will not be disturbed, for instance when parents are on holiday, or when you know that they will be out for a certain time. Accept the fact that you will not be able to fall asleep in each other's arms afterwards, and set yourselves a time limit. Having to get dressed in a hurry as someone is at the door can put a real damper on the whole event. Take time to talk about it together and relax in each other's company.

VIRGINS SHOULD TELL

If either of you is a virgin, it is best to say so beforehand. For a woman, it means that her partner will have to take care not to thrust too deeply or too fast so as not to cause her pain. It is a physical fact that women take longer to become fully aroused than men, and unless the vagina is fully lubricated – which it is only if the woman is aroused – sex can be painful for both. If the woman is a virgin, it is probably best to try a man-on-top position. Place a pillow under her hips as it makes penetration easier, and is more comfortable for her.

A man will probably have an erection within seconds and quickly feel the desire to penetrate. But a woman will need at least some minutes of foreplay and stimulation before she is ready to receive him. This should be long enough to make sure she is well lubricated, but it may be necessary to provide more: several artificial proprietary lubricants are available from chemists, although saliva is natural, readily available, warm and just as good.

The man should penetrate in a gentle but firm way and make only light thrusts, not penetrating too deeply. It is better for the woman to guide his penis into her vagina with her hands and let him penetrate by pushing against him. In this way she can dictate the speed and depth of penetration so as to make it more comfortable for her.

This will also help the man who is a virgin and who may be worried about how to penetrate for the first time. It will demonstrate to him that she really wants to have him inside her, and how to go about it successfully.

USE A CONDOM

In this age of AIDS and other sexually transmitted diseases it is vital that the man uses a condom. For both sexes it is sensible not to take risks with a partner unless you know their sexual history. The fear of having contracted a disease, or equally, a fear of pregnancy, can leave either one or both partners desperate with worry and destroy any sense of enjoyment.

Surveys show that the number of unwanted pregnancies from first-time sex is remarkably high.

This is one area in which you are going to have to be frank with each other.

Choose a man-on-top position for first-time sex as this makes penetration easier and is more comfortable for the woman. A pillow placed under her hips makes the angle of penetration less acute and is potentially less painful. If the woman is not well lubricated, use saliva or a lubricant that you can buy from a chemist. The man should enter gently, and remember not to thrust too deeply, or too hard, too soon.

HELPING EACH OTHER

Recognize that the expectations you both have will be mixed with some apprehension and nervousness. Try to make your partner feel comfortable. Wear loose-fitting clothes that can be undone easily. Fumbling at too many buttons or catches can be very embarrassing and makes anyone feel slightly inadequate.

Remember also personal hygiene. Many lovers are worried about how their partner will react to their body odours, so bathing or showering beforehand can increase your own confidence, and shows how much you care about your partner.

ORGASM OR NOT?

While men rarely experience difficulty in reaching orgasm the first time they have sex with a new partner, it is unreasonable to expect the same of a woman. One reason for this is that the man is likely to climax quite quickly, while the woman will not have had enough time to reach the level of arousal necessary. But the major reason is that for both partners a woman's orgasm takes longer to learn. The man should not feel as a failed lover if his partner does not reach orgasm, nor feel guilty about having pleasure himself. Equally the woman should not feel that she has either failed herself or her lover.

MAN-ON-TOP

Having Ray on top may seem boring but it means that when he's making love to me, he can talk to me, or suck my breasts, which always turns me on – and also, I can see his face when he climaxes. We have tried lots of different positions, but we always end up like this, as it's the way he likes it best, and I like to feel his body pressing down on me.

JUSTINE

*L*ovemaking in a true sense between two people in a long term relationship has so many aspects to it – all deeply valuable and widely involved – that the variety of positions available in our sexual 'vocabulary' becomes insignificant. It has been said that a good relationship can sustain an indifferent sex life, but that a good sex life will never maintain a poor relationship. So long as both partners are willing, however, broadening their sexual vocabulary can only increase the amount of pleasure and enjoyment, and add spice to the relationship.

Even if it is just for special occasions, or in order to discover what we do not want, it is well worth exploring what variations in lovemaking are available.

THE MISSIONARY

For the majority of couples, the so-called 'missionary' position is the most popular and widely used of all lovemaking positions. The basic model is that in which the woman lies on her back with her legs apart and the man penetrates her as he lies on top of her. All the other man-on-top positions are really a variation on this theme. Its popularity is based on a variety of physical and emotional reasons.

Most people consider it to be a romantic position. The face-to-face contact ensures that both partners can note each other's reactions and preferences. Also they can talk and kiss throughout the whole session. Lovers can kiss each other's neck and shoulders all over. The man can suck the woman's breasts and nipples as he rises and falls on her. This all helps to create a loving atmosphere, and many say that it makes sex more meaningful. For this reason, it is a good position for any couple having sex together for the first time.

It is also a receptive position for the woman, if it is what she likes. She can relax, and satisfy her desire to be 'dominated' during lovemaking. Equally, to many men who have a need to dominate

Most times we make love we try all kinds of different positions but always seem to end up with Stan on top. It can make me feel that I'm not wholly doing my bit, you know, just lying there. It doesn't allow me to be as active as I'd like.

YVONNE

In the missionary position, if the woman raises her knees, it allows for a greater range of movements for the man and deeper penetration. A couple can keep full body contact and kiss and talk to each other all of the time.

their partner, it gives complete control – even though they may like her to set the pace in lovemaking from time to time.

In this position, the man can control his movements, and he can penetrate shallowly or very deeply as he wishes. For the man who has difficulty in maintaining erections, and for the one who climaxes too soon, it is an ideal position for controlling the degree of stimulation his penis receives by slowing down or speeding up his thrusting.

If the woman lies in the missionary position with her legs straight out and the man's legs on top of hers, penetration is not

very deep, but sensations for both are pleasant. If the man puts his legs outside his partner's legs and uses his thighs to squeeze hers together, he can increase the hold on his penis and make long powerful thrusts. The woman can use her pelvic muscles to grip his penis, and 'milk' him as he enters and withdraws providing him with wonderful sensations and probably making him climax very quickly.

It is worth experimenting with many different leg positions to experience new pleasures. For example, the further back a woman pulls her knees, the deeper penetration becomes. Try wrapping your legs around the man's back, and changing the tilt of your pelvis to increase genital contact. You will also be able to modify his thrusts by pulling him towards you and pushing him away in the rhythm you choose.

When the man places his legs outside the woman's, it provides a firmer grip on his penis and allows for longer, deeper thrusting. It is a good position for the man who needs a lot of penile stimulation to climax.

DEEP PENETRATION

Most men like to penetrate a woman deeply when they make love, and many women enjoy the sensation of being 'filled up'. In this range of positions the deepest penetration can be achieved if the woman draws her knees up to her chest and places her legs over the man's shoulders. The man should take his weight on his hands and rock forward to push his penis up against the back wall of her vagina. If he is strong enough, he may be able to hold his weight on one arm for a while, leaving the other hand free to caress her

If the woman tilts her hips and puts both legs over the man's shoulders, the deepest penetration can be achieved. This position can be tiring for the man as he needs to take his full weight on his hands.

breasts and nipples and even her clitoris. During that time, the woman's hands are free to caress her partner's back, buttocks and anus, and should she wish, she can bring herself to orgasm by stimulating her clitoris.

Try subtle variations on this theme. One leg over the man's shoulders and one under his arm can alter the angle of penetration quite considerably to produce new sensations for you both, as only one side of the vagina is stimulated. But the man must be careful, because if he thrusts hard and deep he could stimulate one of the ovaries, and this can be painful for some women.

RAISING HER HIPS

Raising the woman's hips from the bed can also lead to deep penetration and unforgettable sensations. Cup your hands under her buttocks and lift her up as you kneel between her thighs. This allows her virtually no movement, but your thrusts can be deep and can make her reach a state of wild abandon. However, it can be tiring for the man – who is supporting most of his partner's weight – so two pillows supporting her hips can be useful.

If the woman is fit and supple enough, she could try arching her back and supporting her weight on her shoulders and feet while the man kneels and enters her from a vertical position rather than from above. Again, this can be tiring for the woman, but if the man enjoys the sensation, he can try entering her while he kneels and she is lying or sitting on the edge of the bed, or on the edge of the sofa or a chair.

With all the man-on-top positions, it is relatively easy to create small variations that produce new pleasures for both of you.

I like being on top as it is the only way that I feel in control of what we're doing. Just being able to see her body and face makes it much better for me as I can see how excited she is getting and that makes me excited. I also know when to slow down to bring her along. I like it best if she climaxes first, and this is the best way of knowing.

GORDON

A subtle variation is for the woman to place one leg over the man's shoulder. This allows him to direct his penis to different parts of the vagina, creating new sensations for both.

By kneeling between the woman's legs as she sits on the edge of the bed, the man has a considerable range of movements. Simply swaying his hips, he can make long or short thrusts in any rhythm that produces the most pleasurable sensations.

WOMAN-ON-TOP

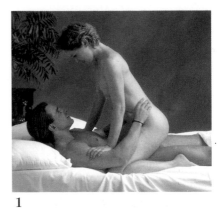

1

My sexual relationship with Mary hadn't been going that long and, to be honest, I used to go on top most of the time. Perhaps I felt that I always had to be in the driving seat that early in a relationship. Then, one time, we'd had a few drinks and, first of all, she stripped for me and then took off my clothes in the slowest most seductive way I could imagine. She was clearly in the driving seat and I just let it happen. The next thing, I was on my back and she was on top of me, kissing me all over, sucking my nipples and treating my penis as if it was the best lollipop she'd ever tasted. For a second I thought, 'But I'm the man, I'm supposed to be in control.' Then she was putting me inside her and pressing her clitoris onto my stomach. It felt so good not to be having to set the pace, it has never crossed my mind again. Now we just share who's on top – varying it even in the same lovemaking session. We keep the lights on and it really gets me going to see her moving up and down on me. I can even get a charge from seeing her moistness on my penis.

MICHAEL

2

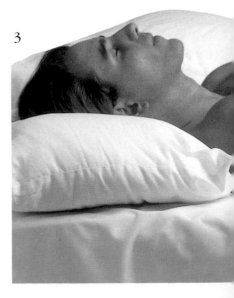

3

*T*his range of positions is important in that it allows variation and gives the woman more opportunities to take charge of love-making. Many men, who often feel they always have to initiate sex and be in control, are actually turned on by this. Before the penis enters the vagina, it can be fun for both partners if the woman teases a little. She can hold her partner's penis firmly, masturbating him while touching her vagina with the tip of it. She can use it to stimulate her clitoris and her vaginal lips. You can play this 'game' until neither of you can, nor want, to hold back any longer.

CONTROLLING PENETRATION

Once the penis enters the vagina, it is possible for the woman to control the angle and rhythm of penetration. She can do this by rocking backwards and forwards and from side to side, swivelling her pelvis, or moving up and down the shaft of the penis. She can

When on top, the woman is free to alter the angle of her body to create exciting sensations for both herself and her partner. She can control the speed and depth of penetration of his penis and direct it to almost any part of her vagina. Sitting upright (1), she is free to move up and down and rock from side to side, while her partner can help modify her movements by holding her waist, if he enjoys a particular sensation. If the man sits up (2), movement may be restricted to a bump and grind motion, but it allows him to kiss her breasts and caress her back and buttocks. The woman lying back (3) takes her weight off the man's pelvis; and by resting her weight on her knees and arms she is free to control penetration. This variation also allows the man easy access to stimulate her clitoris with his hands.

crouch forward to kiss her lover, sit up while he caresses her breasts, reach round to massage his scrotum or anus or lean back to let his penis stimulate her G-spot on the front wall of her vagina.

You may find that the extent of pelvic movement is restricted the further back the woman leans. This can be an advantage, however, since slowing down enables both of you to experiment with the different sensations you can create for each other. The man can twitch his penis while inside his lover's vagina, and she can alternately squeeze and relax her vaginal muscles.

STIMULATING THE CLITORIS

Either squatting or lying, legs back, on top of her partner and simply moving her pelvis backwards and forwards, the woman can stimulate her clitoris by rubbing it against his pubic bone; or either can stimulate her clitoris. She can change the angle of her body in order to vary the parts of the vaginal wall that the penis stimulates. She can also vary the depth of the penis, from its stroking the outer

lips, to halfway to touch her G-spot, to full depth where it can massage the cervix, or top of the vagina, beyond.

If squatting, she can also reach down and gently tug back the
skin of the penis to expose the glans fully, and then move up and
down on it to give him maximum pleasure. This will inevitably
make him climax more quickly, but it may not be so stimulating for
the woman, as the penis will not penetrate so deeply.

To have the best of both worlds try strumming the base of his
penis with your fingers, just above where it disappears into the
man's pubis. While still allowing deep penetration, this also produces exquisite feelings for him. And you
may find that jiggling his penis like this
also stimulates your clitoris..

Woman-on-top positions are also
good for practising the 'squeeze
technique'. This is the method
used to control the time it takes
for the man to have an orgasm,
and it is used in the treatment of
men with premature ejaculation problems. It is visually demonstrated on page
94. You can literally squeeze the end of the penis firmly with
your fingers until the man begins to loose his erection. You can
then arouse him again and continue making love. If the man feels
himself about to climax too soon, he can signal to his partner.

Facing away from the man can be equally sensuous. Indeed,
even getting into this position by swivelling 180 degrees while still
on the penis is a whole new pleasure in itself. When the woman is

To reach the position where the woman is facing away from the man, try swivelling 180 degrees from a face-to-face position. Keep the penis inside the vagina all the time to experience new pleasures.

Maybe I'm strange – but with John on top he would often get the rhythm wrong just at the crucial moment. Just as the first ripples of orgasm were beginning, they'd recede and then many a time they just never came back. That all changed the first time I got on top. It's now my favourite position. I don't know if it's because I'm more in control or the way we rub against each other, but now I get so wet, and my climax is more in my control when I'm on top.

ALICE

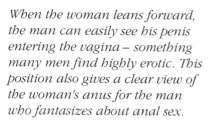

When the woman leans forward, the man can easily see his penis entering the vagina – something many men find highly erotic. This position also gives a clear view of the woman's anus for the man who fantasizes about anal sex.

facing away from him, he can massage her buttocks and caress her anus. Many men find it erotic to watch their penis enter the woman in this position. Although you will not be able to look at each other's face, it is a good position for deep penetration, and also for stimulating the front wall of the vagina where the G-spot is located.

VARIATIONS

In either of the basic woman-on-top positions – woman facing man, woman facing away – there are delicious variations. The woman can sit with her legs out straight, knees bent, or rest on the soles of her feet – squatting. While face to face, she can rest her legs on his legs. The woman can also sit sideways on the penis and bring her partner's leg up to her chest. This is a good position for couples who love deep penetration.

There are other comfortable and unusual positions that provide new sensations. If the man lies on his back and draws his knees up to his chest, the woman can sit halfway along his thighs facing away. It is easier for the woman to direct her partner's penis into her vagina. For the man there is little scope for movement, but the woman can move up and down, sideways and swivel around. Both her hands are free to stimulate her clitoris, and she is alway comfortable as she is supported by the man's thighs and the balls of her feet. The penis is at a very acute angle and rubs up against the back wall of the vagina.

THE 'X' POSITION

The 'X' position, in which the woman lies completely face down, legs astride the man's torso, is among the best positions for female control. It does not simply enable her to dictate the rhythm, but also to exercise her vaginal and pelvic floor muscles in 'holding' the penis. It is wonderful for slow intercourse, keeping his orgasm at bay while allowing her to ensure that she gets all the stimulation she needs for her orgasm.

Remember, where possible, to concentrate on your partner's reactions – facial expressions, breathing – and to massage him or her with a light, or sometimes heavy, touch. This will help you to know when your partner is experiencing pleasure, and how you can increase each other's pleasure.

REAR ENTRY

I find that when we start making love, it is really exciting if he takes me from behind just for a few minutes. It makes me have all kinds of sexy thoughts that get me going. I don't think I often reach orgasm like that, but sometimes when I feel really turned on, just the fact that he pushes into me so deeply makes me feel like I am giving myself to him totally, and I feel relaxed but high at the same time. And the fact that I am totally abandoned seems to excite him too.

DEBORAH

*P*ositions where the vagina is penetrated from behind are viewed by some as perhaps less romantic than frontal positions, but for both men and women they can be extraordinarily satisfying. They provide exciting variations for a couple who make love

As a variation, try using the bed as a prop. If the woman kneels with her legs apart at the edge of the bed, her hips raised and her weight on her chest and arms, the man can stand behind her and enter. He is free to move as much as he likes by swaying backwards and forwards, and can alter the angle at which the penis enters as he thrusts.

The 'doggie' position allows for very deep penetration. This can be painful for some women, and for those who enjoy a little pain with their sex this is fine. But the man should bear in mind that rear-entry positions can make a woman feel vulnerable, and be aware if he is causing too much pain or distress.

It's really a mixture of things. Feeling him deep inside me is physically thrilling but just the thought of him looking at my bottom is exciting. I'm not in control at all, and the feeling of being taken over like this somehow takes me into quite extraordinary thoughts.

ELIZABETH

very often and, because they can be tiring, may be used as a short interlude during long and passionate sessions of lovemaking.

Intense sensations can be felt by both partners, as both are able to move a lot. Penetration can be very deep indeed. The man is free to caress his partner's breasts and buttocks and can easily reach her clitoris for manual stimulation. An added attraction for many men is that they can see their partner's anus, perhaps fantasize about anal sex, and can watch their penis going in and out of her vagina. Many men can also satisfy a need to take charge during lovemaking, and they can thrust very deeply when they ejaculate.

FINDING THE G-SPOT

For a woman, there are parallel but opposite feelings of wishing to be somewhat more receptive and 'filled up' and, because she cannot see her partner's face, a rear-entry position is ideal for her to masturbate, or even indulge in her personal sexual fantasies. For a woman with a sensitive G-spot, all these positions direct the man's penis on to the front wall of the vagina and can produce the most exquisite orgasms. For women who do not respond to G-spot stimulation, however, the sensations can still be pleasurable.

The most popular rear-entry position is often called the 'doggie'

Another possibility is the lateral-entry position. Although not well-known, it is a very restful position for both partners and is well worth trying. Also it is one of the very best for the woman who is learning to have orgasms during intercourse. She lies on her back with her legs drawn up, and the man lies at right angles to her and inserts his penis. Both partners' hands are now free to caress her clitoris and her breasts, and she can reach down to stroke him. Try changing the angle of the woman's hips to create different sensations. Also she can use her legs as levers to push hard back against his thrusts. And from here, it is worth trying to manoeuvre into a rear-entry position.

When I move into her from behind, I feel I abandon myself much more. Perhaps it's a combination of animal lust and the knowledge that she is giving herself to me completely. It is totally different from any other position, and just as satisfying for me. And the feeling that we are both being much more lustful, if you like, makes us that much closer afterwards.

ANDREW

position. The woman kneels down, and then takes her weight on her hands as her partner kneels behind her. The man now guides his penis into the vagina with his hands, although it is often easier if the woman does it herself. Always make sure that the woman is fully aroused and well-lubricated, as these positions involve a lot of friction and both of you can become sore quite quickly.

Once the man's penis is inside, take turns to vary your movements. He can lean forward to caress his partner's breasts and clitoris as he moves his penis in and out. Or he can kneel upright and hold his partner's hips, and draw her onto his penis and push her away at a speed and rhythm he enjoys. She can angle her hips or wiggle her bottom in different directions to produce different sensations. A lot of enjoyment can be attained if the man stays still while the woman sways backwards and forwards on his penis.

A less tiring variation – and one that allows for very deep penetration – is for the woman to rest her chest on the bed as she kneels. If she gets tired she can easily slip down onto her stomach, but then the man will need to take his weight on his hands. In this position there is good friction of his penis, and indirect stimulation of the clitoris and inner lips to maintain her pleasure.

SIDE-BY-SIDE

Sometimes our lovemaking sessions go on and on and on. I suppose it's our way of enjoying each other and giving to each other in a very special way. We often try lots of different positions, and tease each other and totally enjoy the feel of our bodies together. But let's face it, some positions are a bit tiring if you carry on for a long time, and your genitals can take a bit of a bashing after a couple of hours. We seem to know instinctively if either of us is getting tired, and then usually try the 'spoons'. He can play with my clitoris and we often climax together like this. And then there is that delicious feeling as we drift into sleep – one of his hands on my tummy, the other on my breast and his lips against by neck. It all feels so completely loving and, well, I guess I feel protected as well.

CATHERINE

*R*omantic, restful and satisfying, side-by-side positions can be wonderful to end a long session of lovemaking. Whether a couple are facing each other, or the man lies close to the woman's back, nestling together like a pair of spoons, these positions allow complete body sensations. There is always full body contact, freedom for the hands to reach most of one another's bodies, and faces are close together so that a couple can talk and kiss. Adjustments to the two basic positions can allow full and deep penetration, but may restrict the man's thrusting movements. For the couple who want a long and leisurely lovemaking session, they are ideal.

FACE-TO-FACE
Because in the face-to-face version the root of the man's penis is tight against the pubic region, the clitoris can receive direct stimulation. Another advantage is that the man's inability to move slows down his orgasmic response. To achieve a face-to-face position, it is

These are the perfect positions in which to fall asleep together after making love, totally relaxed, with neither partner carrying the weight of the other, and close in each other's arms in an intimate embrace.

quite easy for any couple to roll onto their sides from any of the man-on-top positions. If both partners straighten their legs they can have the delicious sensation of full length body contact and slowly push their pubic areas together. Their arms are free to caress one another's back, face and head. Try grasping one another's buttocks and pulling close together in a steady rhythm.

As with most other positions, slight variations can create vastly different sensations. If the woman slips her legs around the man's waist, his penetration can be deeper and his movements freer. She could try using her feet to massage his buttocks and pull him further into her in time with his thrusting rhythm. At this point, both partners can reach her clitoris to stimulate it by hand, if they want.

FRONT-TO-BACK

To achieve the classic 'spoons' position, a couple can roll over from a rear-entry position. Otherwise, the woman will need to raise her knees while she is lying on her side, and the man penetrate from below and behind. Penetration is full and the penis is held quite tightly by the vagina, providing pleasant sensations for both the man and the woman. Variations that could be tried are for the man to rub his upper leg over and against his partner's thigh, and draw it softly backwards and forwards to produce gently rocking movements. If the woman now rolls slightly onto her back the man can place one leg between hers, rub his knee against her stomach, and press firmly on her pubic area for even more intimate stimulation.

This position has tremendous potential for the man to be extremely loving. His hands are free to caress her breasts and clitoris, and in fact nearly all of her body. He can kiss and nuzzle the back of her neck and shoulders or reach round to kiss her face and lips. Some women find this the most intimate of all positions.

Just slowly, gently making love to Catherine while I feel her body completely against mine gives me such deep feelings for her that I wish it could go on for ever.

ANTHONY

SPONTANEOUS SEX

We were at my cousin's wedding and Jane and I were walking around the garden when all of a sudden she took my hand and nearly dragged me into the garden shed. She didn't even say anything. She just kissed me passionately and started undoing my trousers. Then she leant against one of the walls and dropped her knickers and guided me in. I started thrusting really hard, and when I thought someone was walking down the garden path, I did it even faster. Suddenly, I had this explosive orgasm and that was that. Then we walked casually back to the house as if nothing had happened.

STUART

It is well worth remembering that instant sex is not just an explosion of passion with no role to play in an intimate relationship. Its very urgent nature can build and re-inforce what will always be a unique bond of trust between any loving couple.

Although intimacy and caring are the foundation for the best and most satisfying sexual relationships, there is still room for passion and even, on occasion, pure lust. Instant sex, when orgasm for either or both partners occurs almost at once – even after only a few minutes – can be extraordinarily exciting, not least because the knowledge that your partner just simply cannot wait is, for many people, a turn on in itself.

A woman may need a certain amount of foreplay for her vagina to be fully lubricated and to be receptive to the man's penis, but if she is passionately in the mood for sex this can happen almost immediately. And a man's erection can be almost instantaneous if given the right stimulus: a glimpse of his partner's breasts or buttocks, perhaps under a dressing gown as she walks through the house, can be enough to turn a man on. Very few men are not aroused by a woman who suddenly lifts her skirt and quickly removes her knickers. Likewise, women can be turned on by the sight of a man, often in the most unlikely situations.

The essence of instant sex, or 'quickies', is that passions run very high and that there is not even time to remove your clothes. This adds a new dimension to almost all lovemaking positions. Perhaps the best ones are those that allow deep penetration, such as woman-on-top and rear-entry. And because your movements are so frenetic they create sensations not experienced at any other time.

In the best of the instant sex positions, neither of you needs to remove any clothes at all. The man can simply release his penis

*We'd spent the afternoon in the
garden, when I went in to get
some food ready. After about
five minutes, Len came into the
kitchen. He didn't say a word –
he just came up behind me and
dropped his jeans, pulled down
my knickers and all I could feel
was his hard penis pushing
against my bottom. I didn't say
anything either, but opened my
legs and put my hand between
my legs and guided his penis
into me. He really went into me
deeply and hard and I just let
go. I didn't know that I could
feel that open to being made
love to. He wanted me and I
loved the idea that he did and,
well, it was something new that
made me feel
special as a woman.*

HAZEL

through his trousers while the woman pushes aside the crotch of her knickers. For a man, partly releasing breasts – or even just one breast – from a bra or camisole can be terrifically exciting. For her part, a woman can vastly increase her state of excitement by ripping open her partner's shirt, for instance.

For any inventive couple who enjoy quickies, there are few boundaries to when and where they enjoy them. For many people, having sex in semi-public places, or in a room next to another full of people, adds greatly to the excitement: fear of discovery can be a powerful aphrodisiac.

CREATIVE SEX

Well, we do tend to stick to the same lovemaking routine most of the time, but every now and again we really go for it. Real swinging off the chandeliers stuff. It can be such fun, and doing these extraordinary things together just seems so outrageous that I don't think you could do them with someone you didn't really trust. I think it happens when we're both feeling especially sexy, or when we've taken extra long over foreplay, so that we're both so worked up that we just want to share those extra sensations that you get in all these sorts of positions.

SONJA

The majority of couples decide what positions they like best over a period of time, and tend to stick to them during their love-making. Although there is little to recommend sexually athletic positions for their own sake, they can, however, occasionally be used for a bit of adventure and fun, and can add a little spice to any relationship. For a man, they can rekindle an interest in sex and revive a diminishing sex drive. For a woman, some of the unusual positions can stimulate parts of her body that others cannot.

The more advanced positions do, however, require a certain amount of fitness and suppleness, so be careful, as pulled muscles are hardly a desirable result of lovemaking.

The following pages illustrate several advanced positions for you to try, when and if you please and each one produces different and unique sensations.

The man lies on his back and pulls his legs right back to his chest. The woman now pulls his penis out and down between his legs. With her back to the man, she sits on his penis. Not much movement is possible, but the woman can contract her pelvic muscles to squeeze her partner's penis and wriggle from side to side. She can lean backwards between the man's legs to alter the angle of penetration, or forwards when the man can place his feet on her back. This position can be tiring for the man, and an erect penis at such a downward angle can even be painful for some.

This position requires a strong man and a supple woman, and cannot be held for too long. It does, however, allow the woman to feel completely abandoned. There are two ways of reaching this position. It can be approached from a standing lovemaking position: the woman then grips the man's waist with her thighs and puts her arms around his neck. If the man then holds her by the waist, she can lower herself backwards. The more exciting alternative is for the woman to do a handstand in front of the man, with him catching her ankles on his shoulders. He should now support her by holding her waist as she opens her legs and brings them down to be opposite his penis. The vulva is now fully displayed and the man can enter. The man controls the rhythm by pushing and pulling the woman's body to and fro. This is the only position that allows entry to be achieved in this way, and so provides a unique experience. If the man is strong enough, and can take the woman's weight with one arm, he can use his other hand to stimulate her clitoris.

Kneeling, with the woman on top, gives good stimulation of both partners' genitals, especially direct stimulation of the clitoris and vaginal lips. This position can be reached from a standard woman-on-top position, or by the man kneeling and the woman sliding along his thighs until he can penetrate. It is a position that allows full body contact, and subtle variations can be achieved by either the man or the woman leaning backwards.

*In this position, the man sits on a chair and the woman
kneels 'doggie' fashion in front of him. He then gently lifts
her up and towards him, and she wraps her legs around
his waist as he guides his penis inside. The man's
movements are restricted, but he controls the woman's
movements with his hands on her buttocks. The main
pleasure is for the man, who controls the woman's
movements and, for those men who are excited by the
sight of their partner's buttocks and anus, it is
highly stimulating visually.*

The woman begins by squatting or kneeling on a chair, with her hands holding onto the back. The man can now enter gently and begin thrusting. For the woman it is an unusual sensation as she feels her partner's penis entering her from almost underneath her. Be careful not to overbalance at this stage, and take special care when a climax is approaching. The man should not thrust too hard, nor the woman move her pelvis too much as the chair could topple over. This position is good for stimulating the G-spot as the penis is directed against the front wall of the vagina. The man is free to kiss his partner's neck and shoulders, caress her breasts and stimulate her clitoris with one of his hands.

APRÈS-SEX

After he has climaxed, I know that he will shut his eyes and drift off to sleep. I try not to mind, but sometimes I really need a cuddle before I've come down properly. So I like it if he stays inside me for as long as possible, even when his penis has gone down. Other times I just cuddle up close with one of his arms around me and feel him close even if he has gone to sleep.

KELLY

To round off a satisfying session of lovemaking, it is worthwhile for both partners to understand exactly what happens to men and women after orgasm, emotionally and physically. There are differences, and they can lead to misunderstandings that can leave either partner hurt or resentful.

For a woman, resolution from orgasm is slow as she drifts back into the world. She likes – and some would even say needs – to feel her partner embracing her, and enjoys loving kisses and words throughout this period that makes lovemaking truly intimate.

For a man, however, his erection goes quickly after ejaculation, his penis may feel very sensitive and his sexual feelings desert him. This, coupled with a natural tiredness that comes with orgasm, makes many men want simply to withdraw, roll over and go to sleep.

KEEP TALKING

In countless bedrooms all over the world this scene is played out night after night, leaving the majority of men ignorant of the devastating effect it can have emotionally on their partner. A woman can easily feel neglected, unloved and lonely, especially if she is left unsatisfied. The whole relationship, emotionally and sexually, can very soon begin to suffer.

A sensitive man will at least make an effort to be tender, and talk to and cuddle his partner even if he feels this overriding need to sleep. It is also up to the woman to keep her lover interested and awake by touch and conversation.

Try making love in the morning occasionally, so that neither of you is tired: you will have more energy to cuddle and talk. And try to avoid talking about mundane things such as shopping or problems with the car; talk about each other, the experience you have just had, and how much you enjoyed it.

QUESTION TIME

Q Are there any good positions for getting pregnant?

A *As a sperm has to pass through the cervix into the womb to fertilize an ovum, positions that allow the semen to be deposited close to the cervix, and for it to stay there for some time, may help in conception.*

Choose a man-on-top position, with the woman's hips slightly raised. These positions allow for deep penetration, and if the woman lies still after her lover has ejaculated, the neck of the womb can remain bathed in his semen. However, if you have been trying to get pregnant for some time without success, it is best to consult your doctor.

Q When my boyfriend makes love to me from behind I seem to have much more powerful and deep orgasms than in any other position. Why should this be?

A *A rear-entry position directs the penis onto the front wall of the vagina and will stimulate the G-spot area if the woman is sensitive to it. The orgasms originating from G-spot stimulation are different from those that originate from clitoral stimulation alone. Women say that they last longer, and are more powerful.*

Q When my partner has a strong orgasm her vagina really seems to flood with liquid. She says she is not urinating but I don't know what's going on.

A *About ten percent of all women release fluid from their urethra at orgasm. It is thought to originate from glands that run alongside the urethra. It is certainly not urine, nor is it increased moisture being secreted from the vaginal walls. It is perfectly normal.*

Q When my wife is on top I find that I have real difficulty in climaxing, although she seems to be able to climax easily. Is there anything wrong?

A *The ejaculatory reflex is slowed down when a man lies on his back, making it more difficult for him to climax. Also his range of movements is restricted, so he cannot get the intensity of stimulation he needs.*

Your partner is in control, so talk to her and show her what you would like and how you need to be stimulated.

Q My husband is always wanting to try all kinds of complicated lovemaking positions, but I don't see the point. Is there really anything to recommend them?

A *Using athletic and body bending positions have little to recommend them if you only use them for the sake of doing so. Many of the more advanced positions do, however, create unique and very different sensations in the woman's vagina and on the man's penis.*

Only by trying them will you know if they are pleasurable or not. And for a sex life that has become routine and a bit lacklustre – perhaps even boring – trying different positions can often help to recharge the relationship.

Q Is it safe to make love when you are pregnant, and what are the best positions?

A *Unless you have had a miscarriage in an earlier pregnancy, and are advised by your doctor not to have sex during the first few months of pregnancy, sexual relationship can continue throughout pregnancy.*

Very deep penetration is best avoided and certain positions are best, especially in the last few months when the woman's stomach has grown and it is uncomfortable for her to take her partner's weight. Rear-entry, side-by-side and woman-on-top positions are all comfortable and do not put so much pressure on the woman's abdomen.

CHAPTER 4

THE OTHER SIDE OF SEX

A self-help guide on how to recognize,

discuss and overcome difficulties

together, along with

options for safer sex and your

choice of contraception.

OVERCOMING DIFFICULTIES

*It would be nice to be able to say that our sex life
was always a hundred per cent fantastic, but to be
honest sometimes it's not. Actually, although we're
not seven nights a week people any more, we tend to
have much longer lovemaking sessions which in fact
are more satisfying. I think that when you are
younger there seems a lot to prove, and probably
more to yourself than to your partner, about making
love and having intercourse – and reaching orgasm
seems to be the way to do it. If neither of us feels like
sex we tell each other and we don't pressurize each
other. I think it's because we now have a proper
relationship and know we love each other. I suppose
some people might say that we have a problem, but
I think it is totally the opposite.*

CHRISTOPHER

*I*n a long term relationship – that may possibly last for fifty or
more years – it is hardly surprising that from time to time, sex is
not wonderful for one or both partners. Sex is a highly complex
part of our lives: it is influenced by our past, our present and especially our current moods and emotions outside the bedroom.
Tiredness, worries about work or money, and poor health are all
things that can affect performance and satisfaction in lovemaking.

Whatever you feel, discount the myth that sex should score ten
out of ten every time. That is impossible. Work on the basic
assumption that out of every ten lovemaking sessions one or two
will be wonderful, one or two will be a disaster, and the rest simply
okay. When sex goes wrong, it is best to remember to take things
gently and not to worry unnecessarily. Worry itself can turn a
minor hiccough into a real problem.

If it is just the odd disappointing episode, try abstaining from
intercourse for a few days and you could be surprised how quickly
things get back to normal. And always talk about things. One partner's problems outside the bedroom may result in the other feeling hurt and rejected in bed, simply because he or she is not aware
of what is going on.

More persistent problems do occur, however, and may need
professional help if they are to be overcome. Some may be physi-

*If problems do occur, the best form
of therapy is an interested and
loving partner. There is absolutely
no point in either blaming the
other: most difficulties can be
worked out between you if you
make the effort to talk about them
and continue with the intimate
and loving behaviour that is a
natural part of a successful
relationship.*

*But if a problem persists, and it
is not just a minor hiccough in
your relationship, then it is
worthwhile considering seeking
professional help.*

cal, others emotional; but mind and body are so closely linked that a physical problem often has its roots in an emotional one. The first step in remedying any long-standing problems is to try to understand them yourself, and share them with your partner. There is much you can do for yourselves to put things right.

LACK OF ORGASM

There is a multitude of reasons why women can have orgasm problems. There is rarely a physical reason, but the female orgasm is so complex, and so tightly bound up with the emotional side of a relationship, that many other kinds of reasons can contribute to a woman not reaching orgasm: a poor self-image; worries about work, family or friends; fear of pregnancy; unconscious issues from the past; or simply tiredness, can all be factors.

But the most common complaint is lack of arousal, especially in young couples. This can often be overcome by the man understanding more directly his partner's needs, and perhaps trying to take more time with foreplay before penetration. Men must remember that, while most women find intercourse enjoyable, the vast majority do not have an orgasm from penetration alone during lovemaking. Without sufficient stimulation of the clitoris, orgasm is unlikely in most women, so it can help if a woman learns to bring herself to climax, and then teaches her partner how to do it.

Such a couple can now change their lovemaking technique to include what will make orgasm more likely for the woman. This will often involve a more loving behaviour in everyday life to create emotional intimacy, and an effort on the part of the man to take more time and care when making love. Use positions that give maximum stimulation to the clitoris – or a position that allows either partner to stimulate the clitoral region manually during penetration. But remember that good orgasms are more likely to be the outcome of a good relationship than of a good technique.

Many men find themselves in a situation in which they cannot keep an erection long enough to have sex or are 'put off their stroke' at a point during lovemaking and then find it difficult to climax. Generally, these are one-off occasions and provide no basis for long-term worry. Too much alcohol, tiredness and, just the same as with women, the worries of everyday life, can all lead to failure. The important thing here is for the man's partner to try and be understanding, and certainly not critical. The woman who puts pressure on the man to perform, in these circumstances, will only make it more difficult for him.

Long-term impotence, however, can create real problems in a relationship. While a woman can still enjoy sex even if she has problems with orgasm, a man must have an erection if anything is to happen. Although it may be necessary to seek professional advice, there are things that a couple can do themselves.

I remember we went through an awful period in our sex life a few years ago. I was really tired from work and didn't want sex. Then I started to have these painful vaginal spasms which made intercourse very difficult. It really worried us at first, but Mike was fantastic. We stopped having intercourse and concentrated on foreplay and oral sex. After a month or so the problem just disappeared – I suppose because all the pressure was off.

LINDSEY

The first is to try to discover the nature of the problem together: the most successful therapy is an interested partner. It may be due to medical reasons: a tight foreskin that is painful when the man erects, medication prescribed by doctors, illegal drugs such as marijuana, or legal drugs such as tobacco and alcohol. These can all be looked at and dealt with by a doctor or yourselves. If the problem is in the mind, either for the man or the woman, the first thing to do is to abstain from intercourse, and embark on a self-help therapy known as sensate focusing.

PREMATURE EJACULATION

This problem, in which the man climaxes very quickly – sometimes after only a few seconds of his penis being inside the vagina, or even before penetration – is quite common in young men and can be frustrating for both partners. Luckily it is one of the easiest problems to deal with yourself, either alone or as a couple.

The art is for the man to train his ejaculatory reflexes so that he can learn to control them. The starting point is for him to recognize the sensations that signal that he is about to climax before he reaches the point of no return and the inevitability of ejaculation. Most men learn this during their youth while masturbating. By using the 'squeeze technique' over a period of weeks, a man with this problem will soon be able to control his ejaculations.

During masturbation, when he feels that he is about to ejaculate, the man should firmly squeeze the end of his penis just under the ridge, at the frenum, with his thumb and two fingers. After about 15 seconds most men's erections will subside. He can then re-arouse himself and try again. Gradually, he will be able to keep an erection for longer without climaxing.

Now it is time to involve the woman. She should masturbate the man, and when he is about to ejaculate he should signal to her. By using the squeeze technique she can reduce his erection, and after a while re-arouse him. Over a period of time, the man will learn to control his natural urge to climax in a highly erotic situation.

The next step is for the man to penetrate his partner. Choose a woman-on-top position and, again, he should say or signal to his partner when he senses that he is about to climax. In this position it is possible for her to quickly slip off his penis, and apply the squeeze technique again until he gains control. Lovers should repeat this cycle until the man is confident that he can remain inside the woman without ejaculating for as long as they want.

A programme like this may take place over several weeks and may be tedious for the woman. However, the investment of time and love is well worth it in the long run for both partners. Until you are more confident, try positions where the man is less stimulated. The ejaculatory reflex is reduced when a man is lying on his back, so woman-on-top positions are ideal. Positions that allow

Sensate focusing is a technique to gradually reawaken sexual feelings in someone who is feeling unresponsive. This therapy consists of three stages, and can be accomplished over a period of a few weeks.

The first stage is to explore your own body, massaging and stroking it to rediscover sensual feelings. The aim is to concentrate on your feelings at the time, not to worry about sexual intercourse in the future.

The second stage is to involve your partner. Take it in turns to massage each other all over and talk about your feelings and what gives you pleasure. At this stage you must agree not to touch each other's genitals or the highly sensitive parts of your bodies. After a week, or when you feel comfortable, it is time to move on.

The third stage involves touching one another's sexually sensitive zones and the genitals. Talk to each other all the time. During these sessions one or other of you may be eager for intercourse, but it is essential for the quicker partner to wait until the other catches up. Proceed at your own pace, and only have intercourse when you both feel ready.

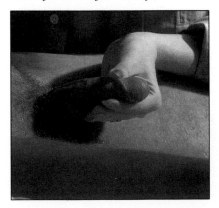

The squeeze technique involves one or other of you grasping the penis just below the glans before the man ejaculates. Use your finger and thumb and press firmly for about 15 seconds, until the man's erection has subsided.

deep penetration, such as rear-entry or side-by-side, can also be used: when a woman is highly aroused the end of the vagina balloons at its top end, so there is less friction on the head of the penis. As long as the man controls his thrusting, he will find that there is less stimulation if he penetrates deeply.

VAGINISMUS

Occasionally, painful muscle spasms that contract the entrance to the vagina can make intercourse actually impossible. Mild attacks occur, rarely, in women who have had pain-free sex for years. They occur more often in young women. The causes are many, and usually most of them are not serious. Poor arousal, apprehension about making love, guilt, inexperience or the fear of pain can all contribute. The man should remember that the action is a reflex over which the woman has no control, and not see it as a reflection of his lovemaking ability or of his attractiveness to his partner. Self-help for this complaint can be quite easy if the problem is of recent onset. And if the woman can rely on a loving partner, she can embark on a fulfilling sex life quite soon. The first step is to talk about it and try to discover whether there may be an obvious cause in the past – perhaps unhappy early sexual experiences – or a current fear of pregnancy. The next step is for the woman to begin a simple training programme.

When you are feeling relaxed, use a hand mirror and look at your vagina. Then, place a well-lubricated finger at the entrance of the vagina and insert it shallowly. Leave it there for a moment and get used to how it feels. Gradually insert your finger deeper. If you feel your vaginal muscles beginning to tighten, contract the muscles yourself and then relax them. Now you can repeat the cycle; insert one finger deeper, and eventually two fingers, over a period of time. Gradually, you will learn to control your vaginal muscles.

Ideally, the woman should next involve her partner in the learning process, allowing him to insert his well-lubricated finger slowly until her vagina contracts. At this point he should hold his finger still until she relaxes again, and always penetrate only as far as she wants. This is usually best done when she herself is confident with her own fingers. Always let the woman control the penetration.

Once the anxiety of having something in her vagina has been overcome, progress can be quite rapid. But do not go for intercourse too soon – only when the woman feels completely at ease and totally happy about it. Choose a woman-on-top position at first, so that she can control the depth and speed of penetration. In the early stages, it is best if the man makes no attempt to thrust.

This whole programme calls for patience, but it is a worthwhile investment in time towards enjoying a fulfilling sex life together in the future. If this kind of DIY therapy does not produce the results you want, then you should seek help from your doctor.

CONTRACEPTION

I used to carry a condom around with me just in case, but I never used it. I think we all probably did to show off that we were having sex whether we were or not. I think really I was too embarrassed to put one on in case I didn't do it right. When I first slept with Sue she just got one out of her handbag and put it by the side of the bed. I suppose I was a bit shocked at first. Then when we got really excited she stopped and picked it up. She kept one hand on my penis, masturbating me gently and keeping me hard as she rolled it down over me. It was strangely exciting and I nearly climaxed right then. Now when we make love it's just part of our lovemaking.

KEVIN

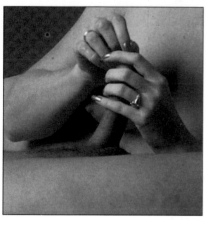

The penis needs to be fully erect to fit a condom onto it properly. When you are both sufficiently aroused and ready for intercourse, keep his erection firm by using your hands, or perhaps your mouth. If the condom is to be fitted by the woman, the man can easily masturbate himself gently to keep a good erection. Make sure the condom is not inside out (1), squeeze the air out of the teat and then place it over the tip of the penis and roll it down (2).

Contraception is, like most things in life, a matter of personal choice. There is a wide range of methods to choose from, but what is best for one person or couple may not be best for another. Indeed, what is most suitable for you may change throughout your life, as your personal circumstances alter. The fear in the mind of either of you, of an unwanted pregnancy or of an infection can have a severely inhibiting effect on enjoyable lovemaking.

The attitude that contraception is a woman's responsibility has now mainly changed, and it is important that both partners discuss together the method they want to use. There are several kinds of contraceptive methods available. Some are for the use of men only, such as the condom. Others, for women only, include the diaphragm and the Pill among the better known ones. Try different methods to see which suit you best, and do not feel too embarrassed to ask questions. Your doctor or clinic will advise you and give you documentation to read on the subject.

THE CONDOM

Until quite recently, condoms were looked upon as a rather old-fashioned method of contraception, but with the advent of AIDS they have become more popular. Their great advantage is that they have very few side-effects or medical risks, and are easily available without a doctor's prescription.

Some couples feel that using condoms means that sex loses some of its spontaneity, and they find it embarrassing to stop in the middle of lovemaking to put on a condom. Less inhibited couples, however, just see it as part of foreplay and incorporate it into their lovemaking. Condoms come in all kinds of sizes, colours, textures and thicknesses; using different sorts can be great fun.

HOW TO USE A CONDOM

It is absolutely necessary to use a condom every time you make love if you want to avoid pregnancy, or if you want to make sure you and your partner are safe from the risk of passing on – or receiving – a sexually transmitted disease. But you must be careful not to allow any contact at all between the man's penis and the woman's vagina until the condom is on. This is because semen easily leaks from the penis during foreplay, and will almost certainly do so if you have intercourse. Therefore, do not put on the condom at the last minute, just before the man wants to climax.

When you remove the condom from its foil wrapper, press the air from the closed end before unrolling it slowly down the shaft of the erect penis. Keep stimulating the penis to keep it hard, as a man occasionally can lose his erection slightly at this point. When the condom is fully unrolled, make sure that it fits firmly around the base of the penis, and that there is about half a centimetre of space left at the tip if does not have a teat to collect the semen.

During intercourse, it makes sense to check that the condom is still on correctly – a long and energetic lovemaking session can sometimes cause it to ride up the penis.

Once the man has ejaculated, it is essential for him to withdraw his penis from the vagina before it becomes too limp, otherwise the condom slips off and the semen spills out. Either of you can hold the base of the condom tight against the root of the penis to make sure it stays in place as the man withdraws. When the woman does this, it is reassuring for her to know that she has some control over the proceedings.

Some couples find that even the very thinnest of sheaths reduces the sensations felt by the penis or the vagina during love-making. This may be an advantage for a man who is prone to pre-mature ejaculation. However, if you find that lovemaking is less exciting for either of you when you use a condom, and if you are both confident that there is no danger of a sexually transmitted dis-ease, then perhaps you will want to try another contraceptive method.

THE CAP, OR DIAPHRAGM

The modern cap, or diaphragm, is a rubber dome with a fine metal spring at its rim to keep it in shape. The woman inserts it into her vagina and places it across the cervix to act as a barrier against sperm. The cap should always be used in conjunction with a sper-micide – available from chemists – spread on both sides and around its rim. After intercourse, leave it in for at least six hours to make sure that all sperm are destroyed or at least immobilized.

3

Take care to roll the condom right down to the base of his penis (3), and that the ring at the bottom of the condom fits tightly (4). With practice it soon becomes very easy to fit a sheath quite quickly, so that you need not break the rhythm of your lovemaking. After ejaculation, the man should withdraw before his penis becomes limp (5), holding on to the base of the condom so that it does not slip off, with the risk of spilling the semen inside the vagina.

4

5

Some couples find that inserting the cap discourages spontaneous lovemaking, and that spermicides can be messy. This can be overcome by the woman inserting the cap some time before an anticipated lovemaking session; but do not allow more than three hours to pass without adding more spermicide. And if you make love more than once, add more again. Afterwards wash the cap in warm soapy water, rinse it, dry it and store it in a cool place. Regularly check it for holes or tears.

Diaphragms are available from your doctor or specialist clinic who will help you choose the best kind for you, help you to fit it and show you how to use it. It is essential to have it checked for size every six months, as substantial changes in weight can easily change the shape of your vagina. Have a new one prescribed each year anyway.

THE PILL

The Pill is one of the most effective contraceptive methods, and in the early years of a relationship it is often the favourite because it is easy to use, extremely reliable and allows uninhibited lovemaking. There have been some questions raised about its safety, however, especially for women who smoke, are overweight or

When we first got married I was on the Pill, but then Peter got a posting abroad and I stopped taking it – there seemed little point. Now I use a diaphragm when Peter's home. It's much more convenient and absolutely no problem.

BRIONY

suffer from high blood pressure when there is a risk of thrombosis. There are also, as yet unconfirmed, links between the Pill and breast and cervical cancer, but equally it may protect against cancer of the ovaries.

The Pill is available only from your doctor or clinic. You will need a thorough examination initially, and then regular check-ups. Side-effects such as weight gain or depression can often be overcome by your doctor changing you to a different brand of Pill. One great gain for women with long and heavy periods is that the hormones present in the Pill tend to reduce and regulate them.

The Pill works by releasing two hormones, oestrogen and progesterone, similar to the natural ones produced by the ovaries. The effect is to stop the ovaries from releasing ova, so pregnancy cannot occur. The Pill method usually consists of 21 or 28 daily doses; menstruation occurs after the twenty-eighth day.

Another kind of Pill, often called the 'Mini-Pill', relies entirely on progestogen for its effect. It does not stop ovulation altogether, but certainly supressess it, and works in conjunction with the effect it has on the uterus, cervix and Fallopian tubes to make them unreceptive to sperm. There are also newer types of Pill.

Whichever you decide to use, again your doctor will advise you, and keep a special regular check on you in the first few months to find the Pill that suits you best.

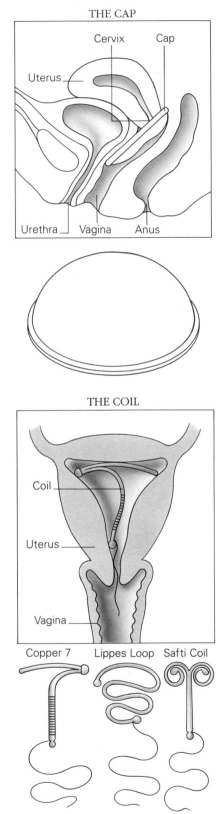

THE CAP

THE COIL

Copper 7   Lippes Loop   Safti Coil

THE COIL

The coil, or more correctly the Intra Uterine Device (IUD), is a flat flexible device that is fitted into the uterus, or womb, by a doctor or a trained nurse. Exactly how it works is not entirely understood, but basically, it stops embryos implanting in the womb so pregnancy does not occur. They are not 100 per cent reliable, can cause discomfort and do have some side-effects for some women, but after the Pill they give the best results. Once inserted, some types of coil can be left in for years to provide trouble-free contraception and uninterrupted lovemaking.

THE FEMALE CONDOM

The latest idea in barrier contraception is the female condom. It is a polyurethane tube, open at one end and closed at the other, that forms a flexible lining when it is inserted into the vagina. Like the male condom, it prevents semen from entering the woman's body, and it also gives good protection against sexually transmitted diseases. But always remember that a new one should be used every time you have intercourse.

VASECTOMY AND STERILIZATION

For the couple who have completed their family, these are now the most popular methods of contraception. Vasectomy, for the man,

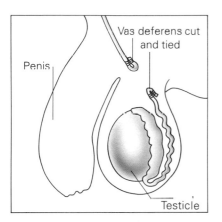

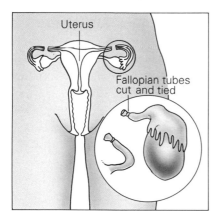

In a vasectomy operation the vas deferens are cut and tied so that no sperm can reach the penis when the man has an orgasm (top). Sterilization for women involves the cutting and tying of the Fallopian tubes so that ova cannot reach the uterus where they could be fertilized by sperm (above). Both these methods of contraception should be regarded as permanent.

The cap, or diaphragm (top left), has the advantage of having few side-effects and is easy to use. The coil (left) is a safer method of contraception and can be fitted and left for some years before being replaced.

involves a minor operation to cut the tubes that carry his sperm from his testes. Sterilization for the woman, involves the Fallopian tubes – they carry the eggs from her ovaries – which can be tied, clipped or cauterized and so ensure that her ova can never meet her partner's sperm. Although occasionally these operations can be reversed, it is unwise for any couple to choose either of these methods if there is ever the possibility of wanting more children. They should be seen as permanent.

NATURAL METHODS

An increasing number of young couples are learning about natural family planning. A sophisticated adaptation of the calendar-based rhythm method, it identifies a woman's fertile days from changes in her cervical mucus and body temperature.

The calendar method works simply along the lines that a woman usually ovulates about two weeks before the start of her next period. As sperm can stay alive inside a woman for five days, and an egg for about two, it means that a couple using this method must abstain from sex for about a week around ovulation. But since it is quite common for periods to be irregular, and all kinds of emotional and physical factors can upset the onset of ovulation, the calendar method is now considered unreliable and is no longer widely recommended.

The temperature method involves the woman taking her body temperature every morning when she wakes up, and logging it on a special chart. Immediately before ovulation, her body temperature drops slightly, and after ovulation it rises.

Ovulation can also be detected by changes in a woman's cervical mucus. During her fertile period her natural vaginal discharge becomes clearer, less sticky and there is more of it. When it becomes cloudy, sticky and thicker it is safe to have intercourse.

By combining these three methods, and using a condom or a cap during fertile days, a couple can have relatively risk-free intercourse all month long. Again, your doctor or clinic will only be too pleased to give advice.

MORNING-AFTER METHODS

If you are worried that your contraceptive may have failed, for example a condom has torn or a cap has slipped, there are two morning-after methods that can be prescribed by your doctor or clinic. The morning-after Pill can be taken within three days of intercourse, and is in fact a special dose of contraceptive Pill. A coil, if fitted within five days of intercourse, will also bring on the start of menstruation.

But it is important to remember that a couple should use these methods only in an emergency, and not as a back-up method of contraception.

SEXUALLY TRANSMITTED DISEASES

Well, yes I have had unprotected sex. Somehow at the time it didn't occur to me that I could be killing myself. Maybe it was the excitement – or maybe it was the beer – that made me not bother. She also told me she was on the Pill, which somehow made it more difficult for me to insist on wearing a condom. Anyway, everything seemed to be going great, and I suppose I thought if I went out to get a packet of three she would have gone off the idea. Well, when I woke up the next day it really hit me and I began to worry a lot. Like, who was she? Who had she been with? It took me about a week to pluck up the courage to go to the clinic. Anyway I was clean but I know I wouldn't want to put myself through that again.

LEN

*L*ike any other part of our body, our genitals can be affected by disease, and some of these infections are passed between lovers. At one end of the scale are simple infections such as thrush, that a woman can acquire spontaneously – not from her partner, to incurable ones such as the HIV virus, which can go on to produce AIDS, and death.

Sexually transmitted diseases (STDs) are not trivial and should never be treated as such, whatever they are. They can cause frustration and relationship problems, but also infertility, severe illness and in the extreme, death.

The golden rule is that if you have the slightest suspicion that you may have been infected, you should abstain from intercourse immediately and make an appointment with your doctor, or a special genito-urinary medicine clinic.

Even if you are in a permanent relationship, it is all too easy to worry about it alone and build up fear unnecessarily. There is no need to feel embarrassed about visiting a special clinic: the staff are used to dealing with anxious patients and confidentiality is assured.

It is quite common to have more than one infection, and clinics are able to carry out the appropriate tests to make a correct diagnosis, and to prescribe the necessary treatment to cure you.

HOW TO AVOID STDs

Sex has always been associated with at least some risk of disease, and the more partners you have the more risks there are. It is simply impossible to be sure of anyone's sexual history. The best way to prevent STDs, therefore, is to stay faithful to one sexual partner who is faithful to you. Of course, for some people this is just not possible, or it can be impractical – if they remarry, or if they have several relationships in a sexual lifetime.

There are, however, certain sensible precautions both men and women can take. Always insist on using a condom – over and above any other kind of contraceptive – if you are having sex with someone whose sexual history you are unsure of. It is advisable for both partners to be checked before abandoning the use of condoms. General hygiene also helps, so wash your genital area and anus daily, and always wear clean underwear. Women should wipe themselves after using the toilet – from front to back so as not to spread bacteria from the anus to the vagina.

VAGINAL INFECTIONS

Thrush, trichomoniasis and bacterial vaginosis are all infections of the vagina. Thrush is caused by yeasts which may be natural residents of the vagina. It can occur spontaneously in women at certain times of their life. The first signs are itch of the vulva and perineum, and a whitish discharge from the vagina. The skin may become inflamed and scaly, and a rash appear on the inside of the thighs. This can sometimes be passed on to a lover who can have a rash on his penis.

The first thing to do is to refrain from intercourse and get treatment from your doctor, rather than try any 'homemade' cures. It is important that both partners are completely clear of the infection before resuming lovemaking, otherwise they can re-infect one another in a ping-pong effect.

Trichomoniasis, or 'trich' as it is often called, is an infection of the vagina. But the cervix, bladder and urethra in women, and the urethra and prostate gland in men, can also be affected. As many as 90 per cent of men with partners infected with trich will catch it. In both sexes, it produces a burning sensation when passing urine.

The woman will have an itchy, yellow-coloured discharge from her vagina, and general soreness. The man may have an occasional discharge from his penis. This disease can be treated by drugs prescribed by your doctor, and it is essential that all sexual partners should be treated too.

Bacterial vaginosis is one of the commonest causes of vaginal discharge nowadays. It produces a smelly discharge – the odour being most noticeable after intercourse. It is not usually associated with itch, and can

be easily treated by your doctor. However, it can sometimes recur, and if this happens it is wise to treat the male sexual partner, even though most men have no symptoms.

URETHRITIS

Nowadays, the most common cause of urethritis is chlamydial infection. Special tests can identify the cause, and genito-urinary medicine clinics are best placed to carry these out.

Most men with this complain of a discharge from the penis and discomfort on passing urine. Women, however, show no symptoms, and therefore may be unaware of their own condition. But in a woman, the infection usually resides in the cervix (neck of the womb) from which it can ascend into the Fallopian tubes – through which the ova pass from the ovaries to the uterus – and produce a pelvic inflammatory disease. This can result in pain and in a risk of infertility.

For a woman whose partner is infected with chlamydial urethritis, therefore, it is important to consult her doctor who can refer her to a specialist clinic for tests.

Gonorrhea is also a common cause of urethral discharge, although it is not as prevalent as it was in the past. In men, discharges are sometimes more profuse than with chlamydial infection. But again, many women with this infection have no symptoms – although both gonorrhea and chlamydia can produce a yellow vaginal discharge.

It is possible to have these infections in the throat, if you practise oral sex. The rectum (back passage) too can be infected, for those practising anal sex, and in the case of some women where the infection spreads across the perineum from the vagina to the anus. Treatment is usually simple, with antibiotics prescribed by your doctor.

GENITAL ULCERS

Sores or ulcers in the genital area can occur for a number of reasons. Herpes is probably the most common cause in this country.

In the past, syphilis was the common infection. But, while rare in Great Britain today, there is currently an epidemic in many of the bigger cities in the United States, related to the drug problem.

Genital herpes is a viral infection caused by two closely related viruses: herpes simplex 1 and herpes simplex 2. Herpes simplex 1 is responsible for about ten per cent of infections, and is also the virus that causes cold sores on the mouth and face. Genital herpes is incurable, because once the virus is in your body it reappears at different intervals. Modern drugs have been developed to contain attacks and relieve symptoms, however.

When the virus is active, blisters appear on the genitals of both men and women and it is highly contagious, with a 90 per cent chance of being passed on. But when the blisters have disappeared, the infection is rarely passed on. If you have had contact with someone with active herpes, the symptoms usually appear within a week. First, the genital area becomes tender, then painful as the blisters grow and fill with fluid. After a few days the blisters burst, and begin to form scabs which may take two weeks to heal.

You will have to learn to live with herpes, even though drugs can be used to control the pain and attacks may become less frequent. Try to keep relaxed, as stress is known to trigger attacks. A well-balanced diet and a good level of fitness can also help to stave off attacks.

One of the big problems with herpes is that it easily makes the sufferer become depressed and feel unwanted or unable to have a sexual relationship again. Self-help groups and counselling services have been established throughout the country to help people cope with the disease.

Syphilis is caused by a bacterium which penetrates the skin during sexual intercourse, and produces an ulcer in the genital area, usually within about three weeks. But it can take up to three months for it to appear. It affects both men and women. Sometimes the ulcer is not particularly noticeable, and in any case it is usually painless. For this reason it may be missed, and the disease only detected when the secondary stage is reached some weeks later. At that time there may be a rash, fever and swollen glands. However, these symptoms too, may be minimal and go unnoticed.

Proper diagnosis can only be made when a blood test is carried out. This is routine in specialist clinics. It is also carried out on all pregnant women, as the infection can spread to babies in the womb.

The late stages of syphilis, affecting the heart and the nervous system and possibly leading to death, are rare nowadays. The infection is easily treated with antibiotics.

GENITAL WARTS

These are caused by the same virus that causes warts on other parts of the body, but they are usually – although not always – contracted from a sexual partner who has them. They appear on the vagina and penis from one to twelve months after sexual contact. They often disappear spontaneously, but it is preferable to visit your local clinic or doctor, where they can be treated by freezing or other means.

They may re-occur and, as there is a link to cervical cancer in women, it is essential to refrain from intercourse as soon as they appear. Women who have warts should have regular cervical smear tests.

AIDS

The Acquired Immunodeficiency Syndrome (AIDS) is caused by a virus, the Human Immunodeficiency Virus (HIV). Once inside the body, the virus attacks a particular group of blood cells – the T-helper white cells – that play a vital role in defending the body against disease. The virus invades the T-cells and incorporates itself in the T-cells' genetic material. Here it multiplies and lies dormant. Eventually the T-cell bursts and HIV particles are released into the bloodstream, where they attack more white T-cells.

As more T-cells are destroyed the body's defence system weakens: it becomes susceptible to attack from other diseases such as infections and cancer, from which most AIDS patients eventually die. Because the virus can lie dormant for so long, many sufferers do not know they are afflicted perhaps for several years after infection.

HIV can be passed on through body fluids, especially blood, semen and vaginal fluid. This means that vaginal, oral and, in particular, anal intercourse with an infected partner can all put you at risk.

At present there is no cure for AIDS. But it is accepted that the virus cannot pass through latex barriers; therefore condoms at present are the best form of protection – other than celibacy or complete fidelity.

TELL YOUR PARTNERS

If you are diagnosed as having any sexually transmitted disease, it is absolutely essential that all your sexual partners are traced and checked for infection – however difficult it is for you – as there is always a chance they will infect someone else.

SAFER SEX

Here is a summary of some general advice to help you to make your sex life healthy and infection free:

• Condoms help to protect you against sexually transmitted diseases, including the AIDS virus, so always wear a condom with a new partner, or one whose sexual history you are unsure of, even if other forms of contraception are being used. Always use a new one, ensure that it is undamaged, put it on after the penis becomes erect but before contact with a partner's genitals, and hold it firmly when the penis is withdrawn so that no semen is spilled. Dispose of used condoms carefully.

• Oral sex carries risks because there is always a chance that the AIDS virus could pass from the man's semen into the other person's body.
• The fewer sexual partners you have, the less chance you have to come into contact with someone who has an STD or the AIDS virus.
• The fewer partners your partner has, the less risk there is of you getting an STD.

The type of sex you practise also affects the risk of catching AIDS. Of course, you will only catch AIDS if you have sex with an infected partner. But if you are in any way unsure of your partner's previous sex life, remember:

• Anal intercourse is particularly risky. This may be because the anus and rectum are much more delicate than the vagina, making it easier for the virus to pass from one person to another, or because injury is more likely to occur with this form of sex.
• Unprotected vaginal intercourse is risky
• Any practise that breaks the skin, or draws blood, either inside the vagina or anus or on the skin, could increase the risk of getting the virus
• Sharing sex toys – such as vibrators – could be risky, as they could carry the infection from one person to another.
• Never share hypodermic needles.

QUESTION TIME

Q Can you get AIDS from oral sex?

A *As with any form of unprotected sex, yes, although there is a lower risk than with vaginal or anal intercourse. Any sexual activity where body fluids come into contact brings the risk of infection, not just from AIDS but from a whole range of sexually transmitted diseases.*

Q Although my girlfriend will do virtually anything when it comes to having intercourse, she nearly always finds some excuse to avoid it, or I have to really insist and then its no good for either of us. What should I do?

A *The most obvious reason is that your girlfriend has worries about being contraceptively safe and avoiding becoming pregnant, or a fear of catching some kind of infection. If you can reassure her on these two subjects she may feel more secure about intercourse. There may, of course, be more deep-seated reasons but these will probably need professional help to be overcome.*

Q I find intercourse painful when my husband penetrates me. What should I do?

A *There a several possible reasons why you feel pain. The most obvious is that you are not sufficiently aroused and lubricated. It is therefore up to your husband to provide you with more foreplay until you are aroused enough; or try using a lubricant. Opening your legs wide and bending your knees can make penetration easier. You could, however, be suffering from an infection, or – though this is rare – there may be an anatomical reason related to the shape and size of your vagina. The best course of action is to check with your doctor.*

Q The last few times we have gone to bed I have had problems getting an erection, and then with keeping it for very long. Does this mean I am impotent?

A *Occasional failures are quite common for most men. They can be brought on by overtiredness, worry, guilt or even fear. If it is only an occasional failure there is little to worry about. Legal and illegal drugs, and prescribed medication, can all be responsible, but these can be sorted out by your doctor. Long-term impotence, however, is something that needs to be treated professionally and a variety of treatments are now available.*

Q I'd like to go on the Pill but I have heard that it can have dangerous side-effects. Is this true?

A *If you are very overweight, smoke, have a history of heart disease, or come from a family with a history of heart disease, then you should not take the Pill. Other side-effects that have been reported are headaches, palpitation, breathing difficulties and chest and leg pains. Most of these can be sorted out by changing the brand of Pill you take. Your doctor or local clinic will give you advice and a thorough examination, including breast examination and a cervical smear, before they prescribe the Pill.*

Q I have never had an orgasm when I make love with my husband. We have tried many different positions and he tries very hard to please me. Does this mean that I never will?

A *Orgasm for women is a complex thing, and something that has to be learned. The best way is to learn to masturbate yourself to orgasm. Then, involving your partner and teaching him what kind of stimulation you like to achieve orgasm will allow you to transfer your needs to your love-making technique.*

CHAPTER 5

KEEPING SEX ALIVE

Ideas and suggestions for helping to

keep the sparkle in your lovemaking,

from the need to set aside intimate

times together to the use of sex

games and fantasy.

OVERCOMING BOREDOM

Yes. Our sex life had just become routine. I don't think either of us enjoyed it at all except for the release of the occasional orgasm. Then, one evening we started talking about how we felt, and eventually it got onto sex and how we felt about that. Talking about it turned out to be quite a release – for both of us, and quite a turn on as well. After that we talked more and went back to doing things we hadn't done for ages. Now if one of us is bored we say so. So far, we've made love in the shower, had oral sex in the car at night, rented some sexy videos, and played dressing-up games. It's fun, different, and makes us feel more turned on to each other.

NINA

*O*ne of the most common complaints people have about their sex life is that it has become boring. The main symptom is that sex has lost its fizz, and that couples no longer feel the same about one another as they did in the early years of their relationship. Finding a solution to sexual boredom, however, is not always easy, as con-

Disinterest in a relationship may occur if a couple fail to spend enough time communicating with each other, or simply because their lovemaking has become routine. Trying new positions, or different locations for lovemaking, can help to revive a flagging sex life. Use your imaginations to think of something new, or try the things you used to enjoy.

I'm sure that we both knew that something was wrong, but we just seemed to ignore it. Sheila would get on with the ironing or something and I would watch the television, often long after she had gone to bed. It was almost as if we made sure that we never were together enough to talk to each other, let alone have sex. It was only when one evening our dinner guests had to cancel that we sat down and had the meal together and we were almost forced to talk to each other that things started improving. We make a special effort now to recreate some of the good times that we used to have. And I think things will now get even better.

ROY

trary to what is generally thought, boredom often has nothing to do with what people actually do sexually. Of course, the same love-making routine, which becomes less frequent the longer the couple stay together, can sometimes be frustrating for one or both partner.

Sexual boredom usually results from three interlocking problems. Ask yourselves: Do we make time for one another? Do we communicate? Is our sex life exciting ? If the answer to any of these is 'No', then there are things you can do to improve the situation.

DO WE MAKE TIME FOR ONE ANOTHER?

In the early stages of courtship, finding time for each other never seems to be a problem. Finding each other's company more exciting than one's friends is part of falling in love. Snatching short moments together, such as seeing each other for lunch even when you are meeting in the evening, are all natural parts of your love life together. Phoning each other for no other reason than to say 'I care about you' is done by thousands of couples every day. But once a relationship becomes permanent, it is all too easy to forget how important these things are – to both. Remember those things, large and small, that were special to you in the early days, and try to introduce them into your life again. Try hard not to take each other for granted outside the bedroom, and you will not do so inside the bedroom.

DO WE COMMUNICATE?

Communicating about sex is essential in building a good life together. It often seems easier at the beginning than once the relationship appears to be signed and sealed. Our culture tells us that once we have settled down with someone, we should automatically know how to keep the relationship going and growing. Sadly, this is just not so, and most people find it difficult to keep sex and romance alive, especially over many years. Try putting some effort into talking to one another, not only about sex but also about everyday life. The experience of marital therapists shows that few couples really understand what their partner feels about things as diverse as food, politics, sport or where to go on holiday.

IS OUR SEX LIFE STILL EXCITING?

A good relationship can overcome an imperfect sex life. None the less it is worth asking yourselves the question, 'Am I a sexual bore?'

It is true that most couples experiment with different things as they grow closer together, and then settle down to the pattern that suits them best. But, as with all else in life, preferences change. With time our tastes change in food, in music and even in clothes. So why not in our sex lives? Ask yourselves, 'When did we last explore something new sexually?'

SEX AIDS

I suppose that our sex life had got a bit boring – and Paul must have thought so too, because one evening he brought a vibrator home with him. I pretended I thought it was a stupid idea, but actually just thinking about it made me feel more turned on than I had for some time. I said I'd try it myself first, and I just started around the inside of my vagina – it was amazing! The sensations were so different to hands and fingers, really exciting. When Paul started using it around my clitoris I was ready to climax so quickly ... We made love for ages that night – it was great to start off with the vibrator and then for him to take over with his hands, mouth or penis. Now we don't use it all the time, but if one of us gets it out, we know it's going to be good ...

LESLEY

*S*ex aids, or perhaps more accurately sex toys, can be used to add a little fun and variety to your sex life from time to time. Most of the ones that you can buy from shops are safe, and it is much better to use something that has been designed for the purpose rather than improvise with anything you find around the house.

Vibrators can be used to arouse a woman prior to intercourse or to bring her to orgasm. It is preferable if the woman first shows the man how and where the vibrator gives her the most pleasure, as the sensations can be quite powerful. You do not need to confine its use to the genitals. Many parts of a woman's body, especially her breasts, are extremely sensitive to this kind of stimulation.

VIBRATORS

These are probably the most popular of sex toys. They are mostly battery-operated, but the more expensive models plug into the mains. It is women who find them the most pleasurable, although some men also find that they create sensual feelings.

Try out the vibrator on yourself before you involve your partner. A vibrator can be used on any part of your body, so begin by exploring. You will be surprised at the areas of your body that feel good when they are massaged with a vibrator. If the vibrator has a control, try different speeds and discover which body areas are most stimulated. Explore your genitals.

For a woman, start the vibrator at medium speed and run it along the inside of your thighs and over the whole pubic area. Try stimulating the area between your vagina and anus, as this can be particularly sensitive in many women. Use the vibrator along the inside of your outer lips, up towards the clitoris. Direct stimulation

of the clitoris might be too powerful, or even painful, so experiment until you find the right speed and the exact spot that produces the most pleasurable sensations.

Now try the vibrator inside your vagina, but make sure that you are well lubricated. If you are not, use a little saliva or a proprietary lubricant to help you insert it gently. Experiment with vibrating different parts of your vagina – the entrance, deep against the cervix, or on the front wall to stimulate the G-spot. Find out what you like best. Some women can reach orgasm this way.

For men, however, vibrators do not provide the same amount of pleasure and are unlikely to produce an orgasm. But some men do enjoy certain parts of their body stimulated, and some find it pleasurable to have their genitals vibrated. The tip of the vibrator placed gently against the frenum and run around the rim of the penis can create exciting sensations or even an orgasm.

When you have discovered what you like best, share it with your partner. Show one another what you like. For most men, using a vibrator to stimulate their partner is very exciting. This is especially true if the man feels in control, and can tease his partner to the edge of orgasm and then stop, building up the excitement until he decides to make love to her himself or to bring her to a climax with the vibrator.

Although vibrators can be great fun, they also have an important use for a woman who needs a lot of stimulation before she can have an orgasm. Fingers and the penis can become tired, while a vibrator will carry on steadily for as long as is required to provide the necessary stimulation. By using a vibrator, a woman can teach herself how to have an orgasm. She can then transfer this ability to either her own or her lover's fingers, or to his penis, so that orgasm becomes an easy and natural part of lovemaking.

Many men – and some women – fear that they will become addicted to a vibrator, and that intercourse will not give the same pleasures. The man may feel that somehow he is redundant in the whole issue. This is rarely the case, however: a vibrator is either helpful or fun – and that is all it is!

DILDOES

A dildo is a penis-like object that is designed especially to penetrate the vagina. Dildoes are usually made of latex rubber, and are easy to use if they are well lubricated. The greatest users of dildoes are women who like to masturbate with something inside their vagina. But they also can be used during foreplay by either partner. While the clitoris is stimulated by hand, a dildo can be held still or thrust in and out, either deeply or shallowly according to what creates the most pleasure. It is particularly useful when the woman requires a lot of thrusting to reach a climax. And unlike a penis, it is tireless.

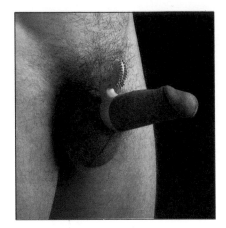

Clitoral stimulators are designed, as the name suggests, to provide pressure and movement on the clitoris during intercourse. They are attached to a ring that is fitted around the base of the man's penis. For some women they can be a great success, but for others they can just be painful or annoying, so always be very gentle when you use one for the first time, and remember to consult your partner about how she feels.

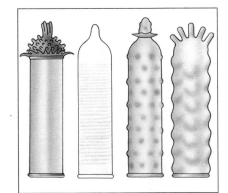

Textured condoms can add a bit of fun to intercourse. For some women they create different sensations in the vagina; for others, however, they have no effect at all.

I've got to admit that we have great fun with those funny shaped condom things. Jan brought a load home from a hen party and we had a huge trying-on session. By the time I had tried about six, I had such a big erection – Jan wanted to try on more but I couldn't wait any longer and literally leapt on her. It wasn't the fact that they actually enhanced our sensations but all that intimacy was just great.

BERNARD

Other stimulators for the vagina are also available. Latex finger covers, for example, which exist in a variety of shapes and sizes, can be used by both men and women. So-called 'love eggs' – specially designed objects that can be carried around inside the vagina – come with or without vibrator units.

A word of warning, however. Sex toys designed for the purpose are very safe, but do not be tempted to use any penis-shaped object you might find. Never put anything that is breakable into the vagina, nor any spherical object that could easily become trapped when the vaginal muscles contract at orgasm. It could require surgery to remove such an object.

CONDOMS

There is a huge variety of shapes and sizes of textured condoms available. Each can be used on the man's penis, vibrator or dildo, and provide a different sensation to the vagina, although many women feel no effect at all. When used on the penis it is essential to treat them in the same way as standard condoms. They are not just a toy, they are a contraceptive precaution as well. Some are sold as being washable and re-usable, but always make sure that you know which is which, as an unwanted pregnancy is a high price to pay for a bit of fun.

FOR HIM

Sex toys that are directly pleasurable to men are in rather short supply. Penile stimulators – rings that fit over the penis with a small vibrating unit attached – are often used for masturbation. In a relationship, they have some use for maintaining an erection, and can be pleasurable if the woman uses them to tease her partner by bringing him close to orgasm several times.

Penile rings are specially made to fit around the base of the penis. They will result in the man having a bigger erection, as the blood that would naturally flow out of the penis into the circulatory system becomes trapped, and the penis swells further. This can have advantages for both partners. For the man, the fact that he has a big erection is a turn on in itself; and as most women find that the width of a penis is more important than the length, the woman can experience new and pleasurable sensations. Make sure that the ring is the right size: too small a ring will be painful, and too large a ring will be ineffective. Put it on when the penis is floppy, or it may be impossible to get it on even a semi-erect penis. After climax, the man should wait until his erection has gone before trying to remove the ring, otherwise in can be painful.

For any loving couple, it is natural to want to experiment with their lovemaking and enhance it in all kinds of ways. Sex toys are just another way of satisfying a natural wish for variety and novelty, while allowing individuals to stay faithful to their relationship.

LOVE GAMES

*The first time, Wendy really took me by surprise.
I thought she was having a bath. The next thing
I know, she's practically breaking down the bedroom
door, and standing there, legs apart, all in black
with her little boots, tiny lycra panties, open studded
leather waistcoat with nothing on underneath,
peaked cap and sunglasses. She told me I had to
do everything she said, and then pulled a dildo
from the back of her panties. I'm telling you, we
had fantastic sex, and now I'm planning a little
surprise of my own.*

GRAHAM

*M*any couples enjoy adding to their excitement in foreplay
and arousal by playing games from time to time. Many couples play
sex games just for fun, and it is simply another pleasurable recre-
ation such as partaking in a sport or hobby. Most use them as
'enhancers', to increase their sexual vocabulary and to make sex a
very personalized activity.

There are three basic kinds of games that couples play: teasing
games, games of skill or chance for sexual favours, or role-playing
games. There are no governing rules for love games. It is up to
each couple to invent their own and to use their imagination in
whichever way they please. The important thing is to ensure that
you both know the rules and agree to abide by them.

*Licking soft foods or different
kinds of drinks from your
partner's body can be a sensuous
experience. The art is to put them
on the parts that you know are
sensitive to being kissed or licked.
Then lick slowly, using your
tongue to tease and heighten the
pleasurable feelings.*

TEASING GAMES

The simplest game is for a couple to have a secret code word that
means 'I want sex'. It can be great fun, when you are out in a public
place with other people, to build up anticipation by dropping the
word into the conversation. An extension of this is to expose parts
of your body to your partner so that only he or she can see them.

Some couples use food or drink to put on each other's body and
lick it off. Always chose something that is not too sticky, like
yoghurt, and apply it in sensible amounts or the whole affair can
get very messy. Lick off the food or drink slowly and sensually, and
use your tongue to tease for as long as possible.

Another prop for a tease game is a blindfold. Providing that it is
not tied on too tightly, it can help you discover new sensations
from all your usual lovemaking activities. Not using one sense, in

this case your sight, tends to sharpen the others and should heighten your response to touch. Massage, masturbation and oral sex can all feel completely different when you indulge in your fantasies.

I've always had a thing about soldiers – or any men in uniform, really. I think it's the idea that they're so controlled and untouchable on the outside, but inside … who knows? Nick was in a revue at work, in a skit about soldiers, and when he tried on his costume at home, and sort of played the part a bit, it gave me a real thrill. He could see I was excited, so he kept going, and while I tried to turn him on, he made out he wasn't interested at all. In the end, of course, he couldn't hide it and we ended up making love on the kitchen table.

SYLVIA

GAMES OF CHANCE AND SKILL

It is possible to buy all kinds of sexual board games from most sex shops, although they are usually rather contrived and expensive. Any board or card game that you already have can easily be adapted. All you need to do is to decide on a points system that can be traded for sexual favours. The possibilities for Scrabble or even Happy Families are equally exciting, and even computer games can provide a new challenge.

ROLE-PLAYING GAMES

These games usually involve some form of dressing up, to give the 'characters' you are going to play an appearance of authenticity. They can take many forms. You can go all the way and hire theatrical costumes if you like: doctors and nurses, French maids, generals or nuns. Choose whatever works for both of you. It can be fun to actually write a short sex play together, working out the storyline, and the kind of people the characters are. Doing this is also a good way of communicating your wishes or fantasies, which may be difficult to express in other circumstances. If you want, you can take it further and record the 'play' on a home video camera, to watch together at a later date.

It is important to remember that any love game should be fun for both partners, and that for most couples they are only an occasional extra. If they do not produce pleasure, then they are not worth playing. And if one of you is shy, it can take some time to get used to the high levels of arousal such games can produce – so much so that the very excitement sometimes puts people off. Always be guided by your partner's feelings, and begin each new game gently: then you cannot go far wrong.

We were playing Monopoly one evening and I was losing, as usual. Then I landed on one of Henry's properties and I didn't have enough money to pay the rent. Henry said that he would let me off if I took my bra off – so I did. From then on I suppose you can guess what happened. Then we invented a complete payment system which included undressing, oral sex and different positions. It really makes the game much more fun and I don't mind losing any more.

GEORGINA

FANTASY

Both men and women fantasize about having group sex, or sex with more than one person at the same time, and watching, and being watched by, other people. A safe and gentle way to act out these fantasies is to arrange one or two mirrors in the bedroom to create the illusion, without the threat that acting out the fantasy in real life could be to your relationship.

We were having a picnic one summer, in a field, on a rug under a tree, and when we'd finished eating – and we'd drunk some wine – we started kissing and cuddling a bit. I could feel Pete's erection in his jeans, when I heard people's voices not far away. I realized this was a situation I'd often fantasized about, making love out in the open, knowing someone might come by and see you any time. I told Pete, and the idea turned him on too, so we got under the rug. It was quick, but really good, and since then thinking about the real thing has been an even better fantasy.

NORMA

*V*irtually everyone has sexual fantasies, and these serve many purposes. We begin fantasizing at a very early age; and almost everyone has re-lived the fantasy of their first sexual experience many times in their minds. Fantasies are invaluable aids to masturbation, enriching the experience until it becomes more than a mechanical activity of release. They also allow us to bring variety to our sex lives that would be impossible to arrange in real life, as it might threaten even the most stable of relationships.

People sometimes feel ashamed or guilty about the raunchiness of their private sexual feelings, and so tend to keep them inside their minds all the time. Yet most such anxieties are unfounded. For a start, it is almost certain that whatever your fantasy, it is shared by a lot of other people. And in any case, remember that it is only a fantasy and does not necessarily affect the way you are in real life – or even the way you want to behave.

SHARING FANTASIES

A tricky question for most couples is whether they should discuss the subjects of their fantasies. The golden rule is: only share your fantasy if you feel that it will benefit your relationship. While some sexual fantasies can be divulged, others are best kept to yourself. Common sense should tell you what will harm the relationship.

If you do want to share a fantasy with a lover, then choose a time when you are feeling close and loving together, and talk about it. Start off with something simple, and listen for the response. If all goes well, you can safely work up to more complex themes over a

My husband reminisced about how the girls wore their skirts so short at school – so when I was clearing out and came across my old school tie – I just had to go for it. In the department store I asked the assistant for some of those heavy cotton gym knickers to fit me. The guilt of what I had on my mind must have made me look so suspicious. So I added hastily, "You know, those ones which are really warm and good for skiing" She gave me such a look!. After his schoolkit treat I told him this story about the knickers and we just couldn't stop laughing.

JENNY

Acting out any form of restraint fantasy should be treated carefully. Never make the bonds too tight, and always agree on a word that means 'Release me now' – and always obey it. Tease your partner with a tongue bath (1) or a slow massage with oils (2). If you like you can try other erotic touches: feathers, fur or even your hair (3). Refrain from intercourse for as long as possible.

period of time. But never tell a partner about a fantasy merely because you want him or her to know you have one.

You may be surprised, however, to find how responsive your partner is, and very often in a good relationship, the fantasies of both partners mesh happily together. But be prepared too for an unexpected response. Respect the fact that your partner may also have fantasies and that they may vary from yours. Women have a much richer fantasy life than men; and men are often more shocked at their partner's ideas than the other way round.

One way of discovering how your partner will react to your fantasy is to observe his or her response to something that describes it, for example in a magazine, film or video.

COMMON FANTASIES

Probably the most common fantasy is that of calling up images of the times when sex seemed to be perfect. Everyone carries treasured moments from their sexual life, and brings them into play when they make love. This kind of fantasy does much to enrich lovemaking, and can be a powerful trigger to arousal and orgasm.

There are several other fantasies that men and women share.

3

COMMON FEMALE FANTASIES

- *Lovemaking with a stranger*
- *Having sex with someone of a different race*
- *Sexual activities with an animal*
- *Group sex*
- *Exotic locations*
- *Being 'forced' to have sex*
- *Sex with another woman*
- *Using a male sex slave*
- *Sex with a former lover*
- *Having sex in public and being watched*
- *Watching her partner have sex with someone else*

COMMON MALE FANTASIES

- *Group sex*
- *Sex with two or more women*
- *'Forcing' a woman to have sex*
- *'Forcing' a woman to have oral sex*
- *Being made to have sex*
- *Sex with someone of a different race*
- *Watching two women have sex*
- *Sex in public places*
- *Sex with a virgin*

For instance, dominating and being dominated, which includes bondage and being 'forced' to have sex, is quite common – though this usually involves our current lover or someone familiar. For a woman who has received a poor sex education, and somehow believes that sex is something she should not initiate, nor even enjoy, it is a great release to feel that since she cannot be blamed for the act, she can really let herself go.

Unusual settings for sex also figure high on the list of fantasies. Women tend to dream of exotic locations such as tropical islands, while men prefer semi-public places like trains or hospitals. Group sex is a favourite fantasy for most men, and although it is less prevalent in women, the idea of being attended to by several men, or being watched while they make love, is nonetheless popular.

ACTING OUT FANTASIES

Acting out any fantasy that involves tying one another up should be treated carefully. Never put anything around the neck or across the mouth, as this can be extremely dangerous. Agree on the rules – the most important one being the signal to be released. This should always be acted on. Use soft materials, such as a tie or silk scarf, for the bonds, and do not tie them tightly – bows are better than knots. When your partner is restrained but comfortable, you can give him or her memorable orgasms by the techniques of slow masturbation or slow oral sex, or massaging with oils – but avoid the genitals for as long as you can. Build up the arousal gradually. The man, for example, can run his penis over the woman's body, or masturbate himself in front of her to increase the excitement.

Next, move to the genitals. The art is to slowly stimulate your partner, either manually or orally, until he or she is at the edge of orgasm – and then to stop. You can do this as many times as you like, but the aim is to make the restraint work for the receiver, and build up to a memorable orgasm.

Fantasies that involve being watched or watching other people making love can be partly satisfied by simply arranging one or two mirrors, so that you can see yourselves having sex. It is certainly a safer alternative to the real thing. Dressing-up fantasies are probably the easiest to satisfy, and many love games involving dressing up are ways of acting out fantasies.

Satisfying fantasies of exotic locations can be impractical unless you can afford the air fare to a desert island, but outdoor locations can still be exciting. It is not even necessary to go as far as finding a park – remember that making love in public places is illegal; try to find a secluded part of your garden.

Whatever fantasy you decide to act out, make sure that no physical or emotional harm occurs. And be prepared for disappointment: there is no guarantee that in real life your fantasy will live up to your imagination. Perhaps, even, the dream will be lost forever.

LOCATIONS

*On holiday, we went down to the beach one evening
and it was completely deserted, so we decided to go
for a swim. We just stripped off and ran in naked.
Then we made love in the water, me floating on my
back with my legs apart and him pulling me
backwards and forwards on to him. It was
absolutely glorious. At night, under the stars,
it was very romantic.*

HEATHER

Although most couples make love in bed, every home provides a host of interesting locations to add fun and variety to lovemaking. The sitting- room is the most popular venue after the bedroom, though it is probably wise to pull the curtains first. A sitting-
room is full of useful props for increasing your lovemaking pleasure. The floor is a good firm surface in itself, and chairs provide all
sorts of possibilities. A sofa can be made excellent use of: try a rear-

*There is no need to confine your
lovemaking to the bedroom, or
only to evenings and nights.
Making love out of doors once in
a while, if the time is right and if
you both want to, can provide
wonderful sensual pleasures.*

It's just great to make love in different places other than the bedroom. Somehow it just makes things special every now and then. I reckon we have made love in every room in the house, and even on the stairs.

ISABELLE

entry position, with the woman leaning on the arm. Her weight is supported so she is comfortable, and she can move backwards and forwards so that she can control the rhythm of thrusting. It is possible to achieve very deep penetration in this way.

THE BATHROOM

This room provides romantic and sensuous opportunities. Bathing together is a complete pleasure in itself, especially if you take turns to gently soap and wash one another in every place imaginable. A good position to try is for the man to lean back with his weight on his elbows, while his partner sits astride him and also leans back. If she likes she can place her ankles over his shoulders. The feeling of weightlessness provided by the water, the warmth, and the physical closeness, make this an exceptionally exciting position.

LOVE OUT OF DOORS

Sex out of doors creates – or rekindles – memories of courtship. In warm weather it can be the most idyllic venue for lovemaking. Part of the thrill for many couples lies in the danger that they may be discovered, and the feeling that the whole thing is 'naughty' can have a great aphrodisiac effect.

For anyone whose sexual and romantic life is beginning to be boring, making love in places other than the bedroom can bring a touch of excitement and 'naughtiness' that many couples need for sex to be highly arousing. And do not forget that making love out of doors need not necessarily involve intercourse.

SPECIAL TIMES TOGETHER

Until we went away for that weekend, I had forgotten that sex wasn't something you just had when you could fit it in. We had all the time in the world and so we could take as much time as we wanted. In fact the first night we didn't have sex at all – we just talked until we fell asleep in each other's arms. The next morning was terrific and we took as much time as we needed. Yes, we're going to do it again soon.

CALVIN

*E*very relationship can benefit from setting aside special times just for each other. It is even more important as the years go by, as most people become lazy about the quality and the amount of time they spend together. As a result, their intimate life falls short of what they would like it to be, or in some cases fails altogether.

HOW CAN WE MAKE THE TIME?
If you have a heavy work load – as many young couples do who have to maximize their earnings to start a new home together – or if you have young children and they take up a lot of time, it is never easy. The important thing is, to make the effort for yourself, for your partner and for your relationship. Try asking relatives to look after the children from time to time.

A few hours together, alone, will be a wonderful oasis of peace in a hectic life; but occasionally, take it further. Take a day off from work, or go away for a weekend. Most importantly, make sure that you both want to do it, and that there is no feeling of its taking something away from the other. If one partner nags that, 'I need a break', it can easily make the other feel resentful.

Once you have agreed a time to spend together, it can be fun and exciting for both of you to increase the anticipation. Remember what it was like when you first fell in love. Send love notes to each other, send flowers or gifts to work with a secret note. Build up the sexual tension through romantic gestures. And when the time comes for you to be together, do not rush into things. Spend time talking, massaging and caressing each other, and generally showing the loving behaviour you used to in the early stages of your relationship. Only you can know whether you want to recapture your earlier times together, or if the time is right to try something new. Be guided by your instincts at all times.

It is important to make a positive effort to create special times together. They give you an opportunity to return to your old intimacies, or perhaps to discover things for the first time, even after many years together. This sort of personalized lovemaking is an investment that will ensure maximum pleasure most of the time. And it makes other members of the opposite sex seem a very poor second best.

I think I've been lucky. Mike has always bought me flowers and little presents throughout the time we've known each other. And then he goes for the big surprise sometimes and comes home with tickets for a long weekend away. I really appreciate his effort and I make sure that he knows I do. I'm sure it's helped us get through some of the difficult patches that everyone must have.

GAIL

QUESTION TIME

Q I really enjoy using a vibrator on myself to bring myself to a climax but I am worried that I might become addicted to it and lose interest in having sex any other way. Is it possible?

A It is extremely unlikely that anyone would ever become addicted to a love toy. Very occasionally, people can develop a fetish about an inanimate object and are unable to enjoy sex unless they use that object during any sex act. But this kind of problem needs professional counselling. For the vast majority of people, really satisfying lovemaking comes from the emotional togetherness of a couple in conjunction with the physical pleasures. Although vibrators can produce intense physical sensations, that perhaps a penis cannot always match, the intimacy in a loving relationship will always be more powerful in providing the complete fulfilment that most people seek.

Q Sometimes when I am making love to my present girlfriend I fantasize about making love to one of my old girlfriends. Does this mean I'm still in love with my ex?

A Probably not. Men commonly fantasize about making love to other women.

In adolescence, men use fantasies while they masturbate, either from sexy images from magazines, or a series of mental images of a particularly erotic situation. This behaviour is carried over, to a certain extent, into a man's lovemaking. Imagining back to a 'perfect' lovemaking session can help a man maintain his erection for a good deal longer and perhaps even achieve orgasm during a lovemaking session that, for some reason, may not be as exciting as at other times.

Q We have been together for some time now and our sex life is fine, though I have some fairly wild fantasies that I'd like to act out with my partner. But I just don't know how to tell her about them as I am afraid she might think that I am some kind of pervert.

A If you think that acting out your fantasies will damage your relationship permanently, then it is best not to share them. However, it could be that your partner also has fantasies that coincide with yours. One way to introduce your fantasies is to show each other erotic books, magazines or videos that are close to them and see how your partner reacts to the ideas. If your partner finds them distasteful or offensive it

is best to keep your fantasies to yourself. But don't be surprised or shocked if she has some ideas of her own.

Q I sometimes like being tied to the bed by my husband when he makes love to me. Does this mean that I'm a masochist?

A The fantasy and the reality of being restrained and being 'forced' to have sex is one way of coping with any unconscious guilt feelings about sex that can occur. For many women, the desire to be dominated – and equally for many men the desire to dominate – during lovemaking is a common occurrence.

Q Are there any sex aids that will make me feel more sexy?

A So-called aphrodisiacs, or love potions, have been used throughout history. None actually works and some are extremely dangerous. Sex toys and sex games can act as 'enhancers' during loveplay, and the added excitement, or perceived 'naughtiness', of them can create an added eroticism that makes you both feel sexier. In reality the best aphrodisiac is the physical and emotional interaction of a good loving relationship.

FURTHER READING

Thousands of books have been published about sex and relationships. Many have become best sellers while others have made a particularly important contribution to the literature on the subject. Below are listed several titles that we recommend to readers of THE LOVERS' GUIDE who wish to explore their sexuality and relationships further.

Cauthery, P. Stanway, A. and Cooper, F. *The Complete Guide to Sexual Fulfilment*. London, Century, 1986; New York, Prometheus, 1986.

Chang, J. *The Tao of Love and Sex: The Ancient Chinese Way of Ecstasy*. Aldershot, Wildwood House, 1988; New York, Viking Penguin, 1991.

Comfort, A. *More Joy of Sex*. London, Quartet, 1975; New York, Simon & Schuster, 1975.

Comfort, A. *The New Joy of Sex*. London, Quartet, 1991; New York, Crown, 1991.

Friday, N. *My Secret Garden*. London, Quartet Books, 1973; New York, Trident Press, 1973.

Malone, P. and Malone, T. *The Art of Intimacy*. London, Simon & Schuster, 1987; New Jersey, Prentice Hall, 1987.

Nicholson, J. *Men and Women: How Different Are They?* Oxford, Oxford University Press, 1984; New York, Oxford University Press, 1984.

Quillian, S. *Sexual Body Talk*. London, Headline, 1992; New York, Carroll & Graf, 1992.

Stanway, A. *A Woman's Guide to Men and Sex*. London, Century Hutchinson, 1988; New York, Carroll & Graf, 1988.

Stanway, A. *The Art of Sensual Loving*. London, Headline, 1991; New York, Carroll & Graf, 1991.

Stanway, A. *The Joy of Sexual Fantasy*. London, Headline, 1991; New York, Carroll & Graf, 1991.

Stanway, A. and Duck, S. (Editors). *The Loving Touch*. London, Orbis, 1986.

Yorke, A. *The Art of Erotic Massage*. London, Javelin Books, 1988; New York, Sterling, 1989.

INDEX

ACKNOWLEDGEMENTS

Eddison Sadd Editions acknowledge with grateful thanks contributions from the following people: Mike Janulewicz and Axis Design for editorial and desk-top production assistance; and Hardlines for artwork illustrations.